# WhatIfEDU

# What*If*EDU

Twelve provocative questions that compel you to rethink our systems of education

**VIPLAV BAXI**

Published by

OB PRESS

PRESS

WhatIfEDU



**Published by:**
Outbox Press, D1203 M2K Victoria Gardens, Azadpur, Delhi - 110 033
Web: http://www.whatifedu.com

**Typeset in:**
Gill Sans Nova Book, 11 font size

**Design and Production:**
Rebecca Grace Vijay (Fount of Grace Creatives)

**Cover Design:**
Andrews GC Angels and A Judson (Fount of Grace Creatives)
Pankaj Nigam (eWorkz)

**ISBN-10:** 81-940482-0-6

**ISBN-13:** 978-81-940482-0-6

PROMILLA

**Distributed by:**

**PROMILLA & CO., PUBLISHERS**
**BIBLIOPHILE SOUTH ASIA**
**NEW DELHI & CHICAGO**

Promilla & Co., Publishers and Bibliophile South Asia
www.biblioasia.com

# Praise for What*If*EDU

*Baxi has assembled a set of wonderful and seriously educative narratives through 12 reflective scenarios which are a response to simple looking but very difficult challenges to the education system itself. I am sure every concerned 'teacher' must be thinking of these questions.*

WhatIfEDU *explores ideas, research, development, experiments and efforts to make the whole process of learning "learner-centered" and not teacher or administration centered. Baxi has tried successfully to address these issues without taking sides, approaching them with open eyes and an open mind.*

*Our education system has a widespread inertia. We have been using the same model for years together knowing fully well that it is not working. Many experiments have been conducted, but they have remained 'experiments'. Their large scale application has proved challenging. I have high hopes that WhatIfEDU will create many 'Islands of light' by illuminating the minds of the readers.*

***Dr. VASUDHA KAMAT, former Vice Chancellor, SNDT Women's University, Mumbai and Member, New Education Policy of India (2018)***

WhatifEDU *is a refreshing and timely work that stimulates the reader to rethink the present system of education. As we prepare for the 4th Industrial Age powered by computers that can learn, this is urgent. Many of the vestiges of a system designed for the previous Industrial Age have to be given up in our evolutionary journey as humans in the Age of Disruptive Technologies.*

*It was a delight reading it. I hope that all readers will find it engaging and stimulating, and it will help them firm up their own personal educational philosophy.*

***Prof. M. M. PANT, former Pro-Vice Chancellor, Indira Gandhi National Open University (IGNOU)***

*A brilliant and thought provoking book that manages to start a conversation about the Holy Grail - our education system. Baxi raises pertinent questions regarding the traditional approaches and makes a strong case for providing an ecosystem that is evolving and relevant, that embraces diver-*

*sity and creativity, and acknowledges individual strengths and perspectives. With its extensive research, the book is a minefield of resources and ideas.*

***Mrs. ANURADHA RAI, Principal, Ambience Public School, Gurugram and Lead of ECHO Education***

*A superb compilation of simple, yet powerful thoughts and ideas to change the face of education. A must have tool kit for all Educators. Baxi's powerful "out of the box" narrative provokes and provides educators with simple to implement strategies at their institutions.*

WhatIfEDU *infuses a new lease of life into our rather stale state of education.*

***Mr. GIRISH GOPALAKRISHNAN, Founder, Wiksate***

WhatIfEDU *is an excellent compilation of all the discussions, dialogues and tweets initiated and moderated by Baxi over the last couple of years. The "what if" questions are very relevant and so is the commentary, analysis and insight!*

*Hopefully this book series is just a beginning of a discussion about the core education issues and will be followed up by much needed "How to" series and eventually "It really works" series.*

***Mr. MANISH UPADHYAY, EdTech Advisor, Entrepreneur and Investor***

*Baxi has made an in-depth assessment of the global education landscape and effectively presented the diversity of innovation in this sector.* WhatIfEDU *makes us realize what has been missed and the opportunities that await us in the future. The lucid synthesis of the vast amount of data and best practices globally are eye opening and force us to introspect on why are we unable to innovate, or bring about higher accountability in this sector.*

*This is not just a "must read" but also a "must experience" book that shall continuously provoke and inspire us.*

***Mr. LOKESH MEHRA, Lead - Research and Development, NASSCOM and Skills Evangelist***

# *Introduction*

***WhatIfEdu*** is a detailed reflection on fundamental constructs of our systems of education, across the world, and at any stage of life and learning. While writing this book, I first identified some of the major constituent elements, structures and design principles, participants and roles, and operations of traditional education systems. The *WhatIf* scenarios were then constructed around some of these fundamental building blocks. The *WhatIfs* were framed in a way that prompted a fundamental rethinking of our educational practices or ways of organization. For each *WhatIf*, I researched relevant examples and evidence of practice from across the world, and also analyzed their radical differences from the conventional systems.

The questions are framed keeping in mind the entire system of education and not just one segment of school or college education. Even where the examples and data are skewed towards school education, the *WhatIfs* may equally apply to other forms and levels in the education system.

I may warn you though, that if you are looking for easy solutions, you may be disappointed. The WhatIfs are not recipes for change. They are starting points for conversation around change. If they inspire more questions, deeper introspection, and critique, then I would have met the objective with which I wrote this book. If they frustrate you or make things more ambiguous, I recommend that you augment them with your insights and experience, to make sense of them as you like within your networks, and to dismiss them if that is what you really want. These questions are meant to provoke, not prescribe, and they may leave you with a sense of uncomfortable chaos.

The *WhatIfs* explored in this book cut across various dimensions of the traditional system. Depending upon how you read this book, I recommend you sequence them in the way that makes most sense to you.

- How do we structure time better to allow reflection, personalize learning, and pay personal attention?
- How do we structure groups so that they are porous or permeable and open to ideas, and interactions, emergent and collaborative, reflective of the abilities and interests of our children?
- How do we integrate curricula such that themes form the basis of learning in the classroom?
- How can teachers engage in reflective and collaborative practices to both learn and teach, in a rigorous and open manner?
- How can we better handle mixed abilities within our diverse classrooms?
- Are we industriously creating degrees?
- Shouldn't we reward every child's achievements and aggregate them into portfolios that more truly reflect their abilities?
- Which new skills and specializations must teachers acquire to meet the demands of the new age digital economy?
- How can teachers use games, gamification and simulations to enhance impact in the classroom, build 21st century skills and adopt new age assessment methods?
- How can we encourage our children to engage openly and constructively with makers in the giant laboratory that is our world?
- How can massive open online courses (MOOCs) really live up to their promises?
- How can school ownership be vested in the people who are most impacted by it?
- How can we wisely employ humor in our classrooms?

I was not at all surprised when I came across several relevant real-life examples relating to each *WhatIf*, whether in support or not. I was emboldened by what I discovered, and it gave me the hope that if I could collect these amazing experiences and painstaking efforts from all over the world in a cohesive manner, and present it without imposing my personal beliefs or bias, it would perhaps be a valuable read. I have tried to steer clear of rhetoric and sweeping generalizations, but it is only natural that I may succumb to them sometimes. I beg your indulgence and critical appraisal on that count.

My experience in this field has left me infinitely humbled because I have had the privilege to learn from all the great work others have done all around the world. I am immensely grateful to live with the diversity and plurality that I have discovered over the years. It has given me the strength to cope with the abject failures of the traditional systems, and the freedom to fly beyond them. It has taught me to be both the watchful cynic and the incurable optimist, and to rest easy with the knowledge of that ambiguity.

The *WhatIfs* presented in this book are a subset picked from a growing list on the WhatIfEDU blog. So these are by no means the only *WhatIfs* that could and have been researched. There are many beyond those covered in this book that are awaiting dismissal, elaboration, or refinement. Hopefully some of these will catch the interest of doctoral scholars who will rigorously research newer dimensions.

The *WhatIfs* are not framed such that they are the only alternative. The same element could be transformed in many ways. Nor are the *WhatIfs* completely independent of each other. There is no way that a fundamental reconfiguration of one element can happen in isolation from the others, and so there is an interplay between various *WhatIfs* that makes the conversation all the more complex. Furthermore, the *WhatIfs* are not without context, though I have attempted to situate that context in as wide a manner as possible.

Many of these *WhatIfs* are the subject matter of many a reform or experiment in the existing education system. But they don't attempt to answer the question or make the judgment of whether the traditional system itself is the right base upon which this tinkering will be most effective. The answer to that question is itself complex and emergent, depending upon your own experiences and insights, and your local context.

There are many things that I hope will happen as a result of reading this book.

One, I hope that many readers share their reflections and critique on what this book contains, and many other readers engage in a conversation with these readers. This could happen on the WhatIfEDU blog, but is not necessarily limited to it. Find your own space, reflect, and share.

Two, I hope that the community will help me include all the wonderful work that I have missed in my research and also help me correct/refine the details. I sincerely apologize for any inaccuracies, biases or omissions in this endeavor.

Three, I hope this work will spawn new *WhatIfs* that become the subject of many other books and articles. These ideas need scholarship and research.

Four, I hope that some of the ideas being currently implemented or considered for implementation, get a fresh impetus and, perhaps, even policy level support.

Lastly, I hope readers enjoy reading this book as much as I enjoyed writing it. If there is any other feedback on format or style, please do drop me a line!

# Acknowledgements

This book has been ennobled by some of the most amazing people I have had the privilege to learn from over time. Many of them have taken the time and effort to painstakingly review what I imposed on them through my persistent review requests, and have added so many thought dimensions that this book resounds with the authenticity of their experience. This book is thus actually that conversation, which I hope will engage you as it has engaged me.

I would like to record my considerable appreciation for Dr. Vasudha Kamat, Prof. M. M. Pant, Anuradha Rai, Anand Sudarshan, Paras Bansal, Girish Gopalakrishnan, Manish Upadhyay, Mohan Kannegal, Madan Padaki, BR Amruth, Lokesh Mehra, Ajay Batra, Dr. V Natarajan, Dave Cormier, Stephen Downes and George Siemens, many of who took the time and effort to wade through the initial drafts of this book and provide critical feedback. They have been inspiring forces and without their contribution to what I am today, this book would not have been possible. A special thanks to all the innumerable people across the world to whose work I have referred to and who have openly shared their expertise and opinions on topics important to them. A special thanks to my colleagues and mentors through the years who have given me the space to dream and a canvas to draw the future on – Ravi Gopalan, Gaurav Bhatnagar, Shantanu Prakash, Vivek Agarwal and V Sivaramakrishnan. Special thanks to the brilliant FICCI team led by Shobha Mishra Ghosh and comprising Rajesh Pankaj, Nidhi Jain, Priyanka Upreti and Sunita Mohan. Thanks to Sudha Passi and Rebecca Vijay and the Fount of Grace Creatives team (Andrews, Judson, Candace and Alvin) and Pankaj Nigam (eWorkz) for their unstinting professional support in the publishing of this book. Thanks to Ashutosh, Nitesh and Tirtha who have kept the flames of friendship burning despite the oceans between us. To my extended families - Benu, Nandika, Shrey and Aman Monga; Meetu, Harsheen, Gurvir and Maninder Vohra; Anita, Naveen, Pranav and Pakhi Yadav; Preeti, Vikram, Rhea and Ashwajeet Bhatia and Fauzia, Lubna, Sheeza and the Zaidis. Thanks to Dr. Suman Prakash, friend, philosopher, guide and the best doctor I have ever seen. Thanks to Josephine for always being there.

This book also commemorates the tenth anniversary of CCK08, the first ever MOOC, that I joined on September 4, 2008. I couldn't have chosen a better way to felicitate the early CCK08-ers than this. Thanks to all my co-participants of CCK08 and other MOOCs, from whom I had the privilege to learn, and of course to George Siemens, Stephen Downes and Dave Cormier who started it all. And I salute the first movers, the people who did not procrastinate but went ahead to actually change the status quo and continue to do so each day of their lives.

Many thanks to my wonderful cousins - Hemang, Sangeeta, Gaurang, Vidhi, Seema, Bhargavi, Nikhil, Gaurav, Heena, Mamta, Sunil, Amol and Parul. A special thanks to Ashok and Promilla Butani for their love and support. I would like to thank Paripoorna and Sambhav, my beautiful children, whose struggle with the current system has in part inspired this book, and who have been active and excited contributors on many of the WhatIfs. A special thanks to Pratiksha, my sister and an awesomely committed academic and activist, who taught me to recognize and respect the plurality of perspective at a very early age and Upen, my father, who taught me the concept of justice and who continuously provokes and inspires me with his erudition and unquestioned love. The book would not have been possible without the love and support of my mother, Prema, who is responsible for inculcating in me her spirituality, a fragment of her noble and indomitable spirit. To Krishna, the guru who taught me the meaning of being unconventional and to always look deeper, to his consort Kamalni, who introduced first to me Chaos and complexity theory, and to my partner in this life and the next, Shalini, whose wisdom and beauty continues to make my life meaningful and fulfilled.

**Viplav Baxi**
**New Delhi, May 2019**

# *Contents*

# #1

# WhatIf

## the school day was not divided into fixed periods?

# #1 WHAT*IF* THE SCHOOL DAY WAS NOT DIVIDED INTO FIXED PERIODS?

*The school day is divided into fixed periods and students move from one subject to the other in short bursts. The system is uniform for all students, irrespective of whether they need more time or less to absorb or understand the concepts they are being taught in class. Similarly, it is standardized for teachers, who have to break their teaching at the sound of the bell into little units with sometimes wide spaces between them. Some topics may need intensive work in longer stretches, or one on one, or as a team while others may need less labor and reinforcement.*

*Why do we organize our school schedules the way we do, and do we really have to? What if students and teachers could carve out personalized schedules for themselves? What if they could create time for reflection, experimentation, and collaboration, as and when they needed to? What if we practiced flexible scheduling rather than standardizing scheduling across the system? What if we divided our schedule using blocks of time, or alternate day schooling or year around schooling? What if the timetable was personalized to the needs of the class? What if we had the flexibility in determining how much time each class needs, and could use innovative scheduling methods to meet those needs?*

Let us say you are the curriculum designer for school education in India. What you plan affects over a million schools. You have a really complex task; that of planning what over 250 million children will learn and how, and what over nine million teachers will do in their classrooms, every day. Remember that even small decisions you make will have a cascading effect on the quality of the education system and the lives of millions of children. You have many problems to tackle. What does your country need in terms of skills and capabilities in the medium to long term? How will the curriculum be decided? Which learning theories will you employ for maximal effect? What are the subjects that will need to be included? What will the syllabus contain and how will it be organized across academic years? How will you train teachers? What measures will you design to monitor quality? How will you achieve this seemingly gargantuan task?

## THE IMPORTANCE OF TIME

One of the major organizational aspects of our system of education is the division of each academic year into major and minor intervals of time. The major intervals are the terms or semesters of study and the minor intervals are the periods of instruction and periods of assessment. These are further sub-divided into fixed time allocations each day for given subjects.

Boards of education or academic councils may provide overall guidelines on how much time to allocate to each subject or activity. They make assumptions about the number of hours available in the academic year, at a minimum, to devote to teaching the subject, the number and complexity of the topics being taught, the year and level of study, the duration of the individual class session or period, pedagogy (teaching methods) and many other things.

The more expansive the syllabus, the more time one would expect to be devoted to the subject. The higher the complexity and relative importance of a topic, the more it may be normal to expect that a larger amount of time needs to be devoted in class, or the scope reduced to fit the available time. As students progress from one year to the next, a greater overall complexity may be expected. The durations spent in each session of instruction and assessment would then be determined by notions of the 'ideal' time to be spent in teaching that subject in a day, the number of sessions required as per the syllabus, and the available time in a day for teaching. Sessions that are planned in too short a period may be ineffective, while much longer than 'ideal' time periods may require much more effort to plan and execute for the teacher. The pedagogy employed would also need to be considered, because that would add to the time requirements per subject, for example, class vs. lab (practical) time. Things could be interconnected, for example, the length of time-tabled periods may impact the pedagogy employed, the teaching style and the kind of activities conducted.[1]

If the syllabus becomes unwieldy to handle given the time available in the academic year, course planners will reallocate it over the years and make changes to the scope in any given year. They would also have to ensure that the curriculum meets the goals they set out for coverage of subject matter over the years. Typically, these goals would be based on learning outcomes that needed to be achieved periodically (and assessed through examinations). These learning outcomes (what the student should know or be able to do at the end of the learning unit) would then become the building blocks of the curriculum and would be woven together across the academic year. Learning outcomes could also be synchronized in an inter-dependent fashion across subjects and years of study so that students at each academic level are geared to meet the needs of all subjects in an inter-disciplinary manner. Then these outcomes could be allocated across available time and session durations.

---

1 Designing the school curriculum, implementing the curriculum with Cambridge: A guide for school leaders, Chapter 4, retrieved on April 26, 2019 from https://whatifedu.files.wordpress.com/2019/04/271335-designing-the-school-curriculum.pdf

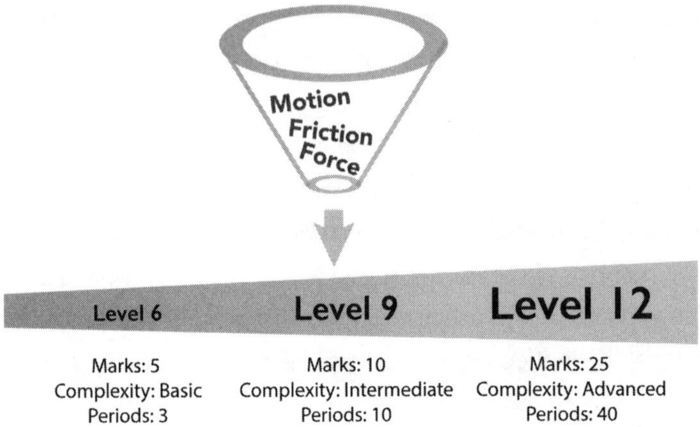


**Figure 1: Subjects being distributed into age-specific buckets**

Think about the syllabus as a large bucket being emptied into smaller vessels of varying sizes, each bounded by a scoring system to determine progress. You could do a top-down approach by taking each academic year and dropping an entire chunk of knowledge and skills in that year. Then you would repeatedly sub-divide that chunk into smaller chunks, going all the way to a particular slot on the timetable. Or perhaps you could start with a bottom-up approach and work your way up to whatever you could fit into that academic year. The Central Board of Secondary Education, India,[2] taking a more top-down approach, states:

> While designing the courses it has been presumed that, given the margin for vacations, public holidays and other contingencies, a minimum of 30 weeks of teaching time will be available in each session for actual instructional transaction. Accordingly the distribution of periods over units and sub-units has been done which is only suggestive in character. The distribution of marks over each unit (unit wise weightage), is, however, prescriptive hence shall remain unchanged.

2 Scheme of studies, Central Board of Secondary Education, India, retrieved on August 12, 2017 from http://cbse.nic.in/curric~1/studies02.pdf

We would usually find designs like these everywhere, ranging from the very prescriptive curricular design to flexible ones, accompanied by an assessment and scoring framework that shapes the scheduling decisions. They may have been inspired by the Carnegie Unit, devised in the early 1900s, in which learning was equated with time in the class rather than by attainment.[3]

Some curriculum designers, like those in the Indian CBSE, are prescriptive to the extent of prescribing even the number of sessions per week required in a subject and the time spent per session. In this kind of a system, there may be limited flexibility in emphasis on any one unit of knowledge and limited manipulation of subject sessions (double periods, extra classes, balances 'heavy' vs. 'lighter' subjects in a day). Also, teachers do consider their own availability, and the ground level student and time scenarios, and adapt the timetable accordingly. In general, these guidelines shape the way in which timetables are initially conceived and structured.

The more flexible designers would set broad goals at each stage of education and provide a lot of freedom to teachers and institutions to frame the actual implementation. Teachers would be relatively more autonomous. They would have the flexibility to interpret the curriculum and manage scheduling in a way that best meets the overall requirements.

## THE SYSTEM AT SCALE

Being prescriptive increases manageability at scale. The less the individual variance at each level in the system, the more streamlined the monitoring of learning outcomes can be. Simply put, such a curriculum with limited flexibility makes it easy to manage and monitor learning outcomes in a large education system such as in India. On the other hand, if the curriculum is more broad-based and allows more teacher creativity or innovation, or curricular flexibility, the planners would

3 Harris, John (2002). Brief history of American academic credit system, a recipe for incoherence in student learning, retrieved on August 4, 2018 from http://files.eric.ed.gov/fulltext/ED470030.pdf

need to balance that flexibility with being more prescriptive with the examination structure. This is required in order to scale reliably and consistently in terms of metrics like pass rates, scores, and attendance.

Overall, the system seems to be able to operate at scale only if it is able to balance between the curricular goals and the available time. By scale, we mean the ability of the system to work efficiently even with large numbers of students, groups, topics and activities. It is an industry-like problem that may require complex timetabling software to solve efficiently and reliably.

It would work well, were it not so complicated. There are two types of issues here – the ones that concern the use and abuse of the system as it is designed, and the ones that occur in its implementation.

In the framing or design of the system, many issues may be encountered. Overloads may occur in terms of the time allocated for coverage of the syllabus. Units may be awarded misplaced weights. Irrelevant units may be included and more useful ones excluded. The curriculum may also suffer from its own pedagogical or andragogical[4] limitations, for example, with its tilt towards rote learning.

An interesting example is the Delhi state government, which realized that up to 25 percent of the curriculum for grades 1-8 was not even transacted by teachers because of the paucity of time.[5] Director, Education, Padmini Singla explained that no part of the syllabus that is crucial to the children's understanding of concepts has been removed. 'They weren't completing all the chapters in the book anyway. We're just reducing them. The sections were selected by an internal committee which had members from the SCERT (State Council of Educational Research and Training) as well,' she said.[6]

---

4 Andragogy refers to the principles, methods and techniques of adult education. Malcolm Knowles developed a theory of education that addressed how adults learn. See more at http://infed.org/mobi/andragogy-what-is-it-and-does-it-help-thinking-about-adult-learning/.

5 Baxi, Viplav (2015, September 8). Delhi's syllabus haircut, retrieved on November 1, 2017 from https://learnos.wordpress.com/2015/09/08/delhis-syllabus-haircut/

6 The Times of India (2015, September 5). Lighter bags for kids as govt to cut syllabi, *The Times of India*, retrieved on November 1, 2017 from http://timesofindia.indiatimes.com/city/delhi/Lighter-bags-for-kids-as-govt-to-cut-syllabi/articleshow/48839917.cms

Following on this initiative, the Indian government has announced plans to cut the syllabus by half since students are overburdened and do not get time for "physical education, value education and life skills."[7] In fact, the government is considering a host of other measures including unifying the curriculum and introducing more standardized testing across the nation.

It could have been that the syllabus was too exhaustive to start with and should have been reduced anyway. Or, it could result in dumbing down the system by excluding content which although seems superfluous, is actually required for subsequent levels. This move could also result in downstream effects, when the nation goes through standardized national testing for the major education boards, in classes 10 and 12. Whatever be the reasons for this action, it clearly demonstrates that either the curriculum planners were off the mark by 25-50 percent or that the implementation of the curriculum had a 25-50 percent gap, or perhaps a combination of both.

In the implementation of the scheduling system, there will always be issues – what is designed may not be implemented with high scrupulousness across every instance of its occurrence. The causes may lie in teacher skills, availability, adapting to best practices, permissive exam practices, lack of infrastructure, deficient analytics, absence of personalization, and many such causes.

More importantly, we assume that such a system is suited for scale. We assume that this common-sense, almost industrial approach, is perhaps the only way things can operate efficiently. This is perhaps one common-sense way of organizing instruction, but is it a common-sense way of organizing learning? It may be a common-sense way for allocating teacher time, for managing scarce institutional resources and for administering a fixed assessment system, but can it really handle the diversity and depth in our education systems?

---

7 Economic Times (2018). Students are overburdened, NCERT syllabus to be cut to half: HRD minister, retrieved on June 11, 2018 from https://economictimes.indiatimes.com/industry/services/education/government-decided-to-reduce-ncert-syllabus-as-students-are-overburdened-hrd-minister/articleshow/64482658.cms

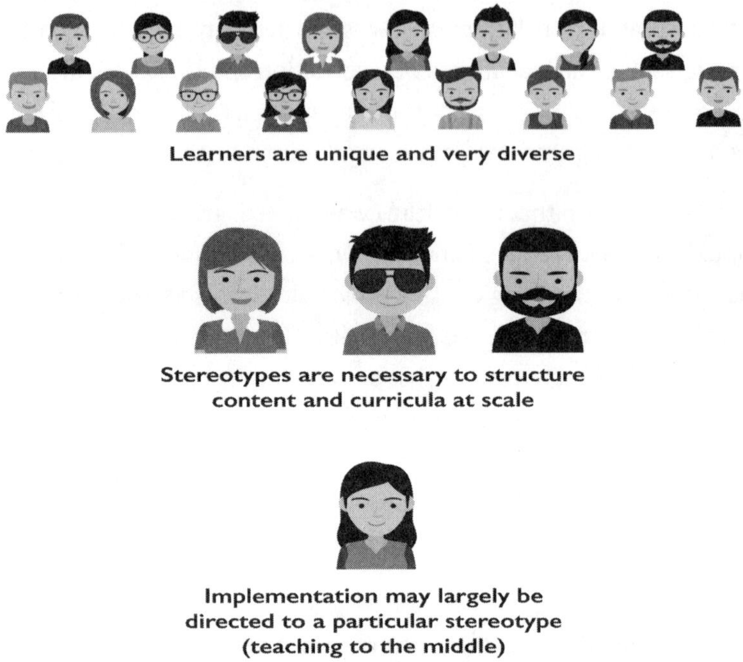


**Figure 2: Teaching to the middle**

This approach isn't scalable, really, unless you approach scaling as a way to enforce, for good or bad, a system that makes students and teachers common, rather than special. This is because to create and implement a design based on this assumption of scalability, many other assumptions have to necessarily be made. For example, let us consider how we handle diversity across students, teachers and institutions through implicitly or explicitly defined stereotypes.

Stereotypes of students, for example, 'fast' vs. 'slow' learners or visual/auditory/kinesthetic[8] learners, suppress their individual differences. Stereotypes of teachers aggregate and simplify the wide diversity of skills, attitudes, and behaviors of teachers through the system. Institutions also

8 A kinesthetic learner is one who learns by physically participating in creating or doing something, rather than being a passive recipient, and listening to or watching something. The visual learner has a preference for learning through what they can see and visualize, while the auditory learner likes to learn by talking and listening.

are stereotyped in terms of their ownership, infrastructure, and other norms. These stereotypes are necessary to design a scalable structure and determine the standard processes of learning and teaching.

## SCALING WITH QUALITY

So what if we decided that this common-sense solution would be replaced or improved by another scalable solution that respects individual creativity, interest and learning ability, and merges that with our conception of vital knowledge and skills that ought to be demonstrable in some form? Basically can we shift our attention away from this curricular preoccupation with what is to be taught and when, towards allowing individual teachers and students to develop the initiative, commitment, passion, grit, knowledge and skills they need to negotiate teaching and learning? Let us look at some of the innovations and alternatives in session scheduling that can enable this shift.

Joseph Carroll, an educator and administrator, worked across many schools and school districts in the United States of America. One of his assignments was as the Superintendent for Research, Budget and Legislation for the District of Columbia Public Schools. At that time, children aged around 13 years had to compulsorily make a transition from elementary to the more demanding junior school. This was irrespective of their individual levels of academic attainment. He devised a 6-week summer program to help children make this transition. They would come in for four hours each day and study math and reading. He found that an average student progressed two or three grade levels in this program. But when the students returned to regular school schedules, many of these gains were erased.

In 1969, when he moved to become the Superintendent of the Los Alamos, New Mexico Public Schools, he found that students who spent four hours a day on a course in chemistry or math, five days a week for six weeks (a total of 120 hours) learnt as well as students who were taught the course in 180 50-minute sessions through the year (a total of 150 hours).

He began calling this more compact structure, 'macro-scheduling.' In 1983, he took this idea along with his ideas on mastery learning, to create the first draft of what he called the Copernican Plan.[9] Instead of students having to change locations, subjects, and activities seven to nine times each day, they concentrated on one or two subjects at a time, each taught in an extended 'macro-class.'

Carroll's proposal was to have students engage with one subject at a time for four hours a day for 30 days. Each student would enroll in six of these classes every year, making a total of the required 180 days of schooling. Students could alternatively enroll for two two-hour classes for 60 days as part of a trimester plan. Schools could have six and twelve week courses run together as well. In the block of time freed up each day using this method, seminars would be arranged that could focus on bringing out the inter-disciplinary nature of courses. Teachers could then focus on developing and implementing strategies for personalized instruction rather than teaching to the 'intellectual middle.' The number of students they met each day would be substantially reduced as compared to the number of students they encountered moving from class to class, teaching five subjects a day. By teaching six classes instead of five as in the original scheme, they would reduce their class size by at least 20 percent and drop their daily student load by 60 percent (even if they had two two-hour classes for a trimester course), because they would be dealing with a smaller number of students over larger periods each day. They would, therefore, be able to spend more quality time with those students that needed it. They would get more time to plan, to address individual differences, to mark homework and many other things.

---

9 Carroll, Joseph M (1989). The Copernican plan: restructuring the American high school, retrieved on December 11, 2017 from https://files.eric.ed.gov/fulltext/ED313812.pdf

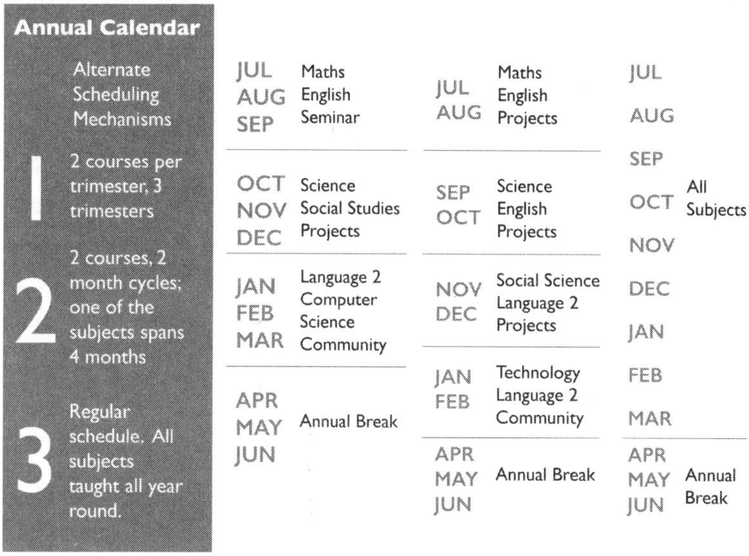


**Figure 3: Alternate course scheduling mechanisms**

Block Scheduling was a proposal inspired by Joseph Carroll's Copernican model:[10]

> In the ***alternate-day*** schedule students and teachers meet every other-day for extended time periods rather than meeting every day for shorter periods.
>
> In the *4/4 semester plan* students complete four "year-long" courses that meet for about 90 minutes every day during a 90-day semester.
>
> Students take *two or three courses every 60 days* in a trimester plan to earn six to nine credits per year.

This type of scheduling has many benefits – less fragmentation of students' attention, less chaos between classes, more time for activities other than pure lecture time, greater attention to students' needs and reduced record-keeping. It allows students and teachers to devote more

10 Cromwell, Sharon (1997, October 20). Block scheduling: A solution or a problem, retrieved on August 13, 2017 from http://www.educationworld.com/a_admin/admin/admin029.shtml

time together in joint activity, allows far greater interaction, provides space for team-based activities, and even one to one guidance. Team teaching is also made possible in such scenarios. But it may also have challenges if not handled correctly, such as not being able to effectively handle low attention spans and not having mechanisms for students to make up for missed classes. Low attention spans are often quoted as a challenge, but it is possible to retain students on a topic for longer intervals by redesigning our teaching methods.

A review of research[11] does not show a decisively clear verdict for or against the system. But the point being made is that this innovation only reinforces the notion that time is an important component of the system that deserves far more attention.

The National Center on Time and Learning, a Boston based non-profit,[12] focuses on just these kinds of questions.

> It's time to change the way we think about the school day. Redesigning and significantly expanding the school day can give students nearly two additional years of learning time. When done well, expanding learning time raises achievement, enriches education and empowers teachers.

Administrators and curriculum planners would want a predictable model to achieve their stated outcomes. Changing the way we manage time may introduce chaos. At what point will these alternatives and improvements in the system get so chaotic that they defeat the very outcomes we want? We need to control this disorder creatively, tweaking or transforming other parts of the system such that they start supporting this change.

Looked at another way, let us say that we are asking our children to spend upwards of 12,000-15,000 hours of their lives in school and at

---

11 Dickson Kelly, Karen Bird, Mark Newman, and Naira Kalra (2010). What is the effect of block scheduling on academic achievement? A systematic review, Report no. 1802R, February 2010, EPPI-Centre, Social Science Research Unit, Institute of Education, University of London, retrieved on 13 August 2017 from http://eppi.ioe.ac.uk/cms/Portals/0/PDF%20reviews%20and%20summaries/Block%20scheduling%20Report.pdf?ver=2010-02-24-160528-010

12 Why expand learning time, National Center on Time and Learning, USA, retrieved on August 13, 2017 from http://timeandlearning.org/why-more-school-time

home on a system of education that we have conceived (or notionally about 2500-3000 hours per subject over 12 years of schooling). Can this time be better organized?

As a case in point, what if the system involved a time-table to be created every week on the basis of the results of the preceding week? If this is a desirable change, then what other parts of the system will need to be changed to accommodate this change?

## USING TIME BETTER

The Swedish Kunskapsskolan KED[13] initiative provides some insight into how this can be made possible. Even though they formally conform to certain educational boards, they break from tradition in a number of ways, by rethinking time. A typical day[14] starts with students meeting their 'base' group and coach. They perform an activity as a group (like watching the daily news) and then the teacher helps students create their personalized time plans. During the day students attend different activities such as lectures, workshops, seminars and communication sessions. Students get personalized support when starting a new course or to help improve their learning skills.

Experiments like the AltSchool[15] also show glimpses of what else may need to change in the system if time is to be reconsidered.

> The pedagogical model is a modern, technology-supported spin on Montessori, with students learning together through interdisciplinary projects while mastering core knowledge and skills at their own pace, via a personalized sequence of digital curricula. Mornings are typically skill-based, with students progressing through structured online lessons

13 History, Kunskappskolan, retrieved on November 1, 2017 from http://ked.edu.in/introduction/history/

14 A day at Kunskappsskolan, retrieved on November 1, 2017 from http://ked.edu.in/our-flagship-school/a-day-at-kunskapsskolan/

15 Inside NYC's very first AltSchool, the tech-driven startup that's rethinking American education, *THE74*, retrieved on August 13, 2017 from https://www.the74million.org/article/inside-nycs-very-first-altschool-the-tech-driven-startup-thats-rethinking-american-education

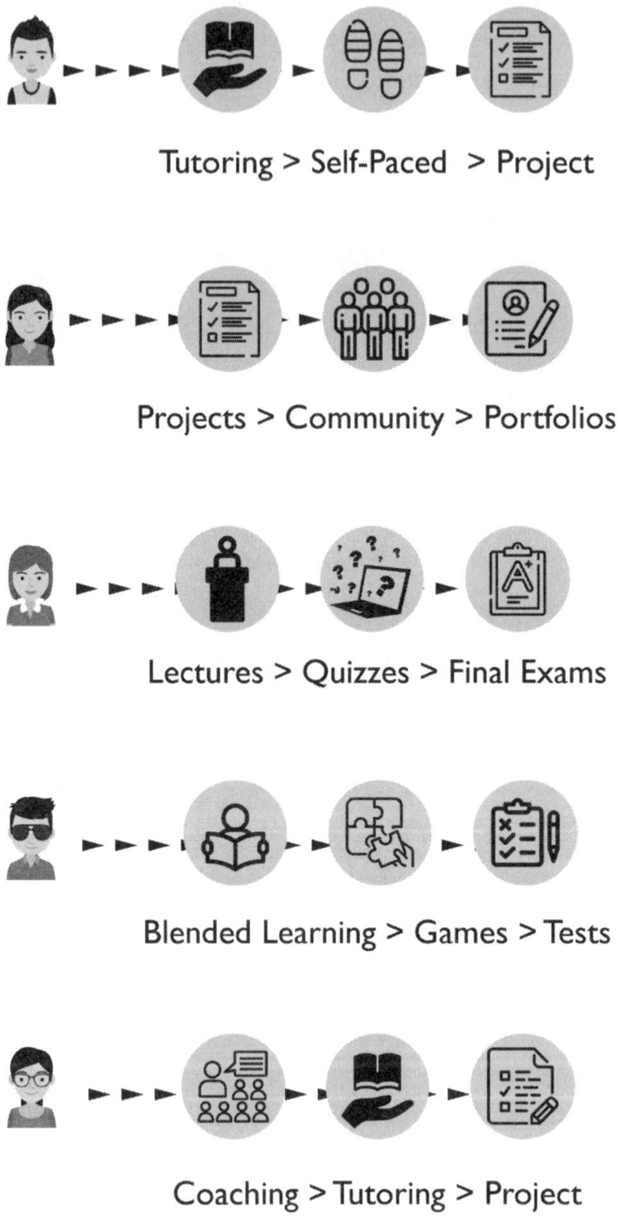


**Figure 4: Dynamic, adaptive timetables personalized for the student**

> in core subjects like math and reading. Later in the day, students turn to planned activities and longer-term projects with teachers playing a variety of roles—tutor, coach, community organizer—throughout.

The pilot Khan Lab[16] schools also espouse a more student oriented and technology enabled conception of time.

> Every week, students set their own academic goals—the level of math they hope to master, the amount of time they plan to dedicate to reading, and so on. Over the course of the week, they use Khan Academy and other self-directed educational software to try to accomplish those goals.

Or we could take a look at the Atma Vidya Educational Foundation (AVEF),[17] whose school in Kerala has been quoted as one of the top 10 most innovative schools in India, which goes a step further.

> In an environment of guided freedom, the school's curriculum is introduced to the children without textbooks or examinations until eighth standard, placing the responsibility on the teacher of finding ways to introduce subject matter through children's interests. The children naturally learn in an interdisciplinary way and make connections among subjects.

The AVEF philosophy is to build on individual choice and the relook at the relationship between the teacher and the student. The school provides an environment of choice shaping itself according to the needs and interests of the child at one end, and the formal educational board examination requirements at the other.

Malcolm Gladwell has proposed that to become an expert at anything, one needs to spend upwards of 10,000 hours (*the magic number of*

---

16 Tanz, Jason (2015, October 26). The tech elite's quest to reinvent school in its own image, *Wired*, retrieved on August 3, 2018 from https://khanlabschool.org/wired

17 Atma Vidya Educational Foundation, https://alliance-edu-foundation.org

*greatness*) or 90 minutes practice a day for 20 years[18] (critics have stated that the quality of practice was more important and that this 'magic number' is too simplistic).[19] Of course, he is talking about professional expertise, which goes beyond what is thought to be achieved at school, but we could expect that these 12-15,000 hours that students spend could be well spent if, for example, students became expert learners – learners who by sheer reflection and practice, by the dint of highly developed meta-cognitive skills, became expert at acquiring, applying, and extending knowledge.

In many forms of creative arts, the student is ready for the next level when she is 'deemed' to be ready by someone – a guru or an award-giving group or association. Often, getting a pupil 'ready' takes a long time and several cycles of shared failures and successes. Instead of regimenting these cycles to be a precious few instances limited by the division of time, what if we allow timetables to evolve through any given time interval based on student and teacher choice, learning abilities, interests and other factors?

In sports, a similar system of grooming individual talent and team performance is the default model. Coaches and mentors don't only teach concepts, but also help each individual student to reach their maximum potential in a systematic manner. They too have a framework of assessment based on success in competitions and techniques that help them achieve that at scale. Again, they have adjusted the scale and rate of instruction based on multiple student factors.

There are many more examples of flexible scheduling throughout the world that could be explored for their perspective on time. These discussions may help trigger a re-conceptualization of our current ideas

---

18 Gladwell, Malcolm (2008). *Outliers: The story of success*, Back Bay Books

19 Nightingale, Rob (2015, December 9). The 10,000 hour rule is wrong. How to really master a skill, retrieved on August 13, 2017 from http://www.makeuseof.com/tag/10000-hour-rule-wrong-really-master-skill/

of time in the education system, at scale. Tweaking our conception of time will also invariably prompt a reconfiguration of other aspects of the system such as curriculum, pedagogy, teacher education and almost everything else. But it is an interesting point to start from, an interesting question to ask!

# #2

# What*If*

## school was not divided into classes and sections?

# #2 WHAT*IF* SCHOOL WAS NOT DIVIDED INTO CLASSES AND SECTIONS?

*The present day organization of an education system is based on periods of study and segmentation of students into sections or groups. Many of us have grown up accepting this structure of the school system and perhaps never given a second thought to it. Is this the only way or the most optimal way that schooling could be organized?*

*After all, why is twelve years or sixteen years of schooling mandatory? Why is the duration of a Bachelor's degree three or four years? What if school ran all year round rather than (say) 30 weeks in a year? What if we extended or shortened the school day? What if we had alternating school weeks, one for teaching and the other at home or activity centers for project work and reinforcement?*

*Within an academic period of study like a school class/year, why do we break students up into sub-groups (sections or batches)? What if did not follow this division into groups? What determines our decisions of putting certain students in one section or the other? How do we determine who makes it to a class at all? What would happen if we changed the definitions of the groups and their progression?*

Imagine the role of a board of education that affiliates a large number of schools. Their job is to define the administrative process and guidelines across their affiliate schools. They have made the decision that schooling will be divided into twelve grades, each spanning an entire year. At the end of each year, they have defined exit examinations to determine which student makes it to the next grade. That also means that they have defined the admission criteria for any grade level. This could be a combination of age, location, previous performance, and other factors.

As the school administrator of a school affiliated to this board, you would then conduct the admissions and promotions processes according to the board's rules. The exact number of students you will admit at a particular grade level would depend on which grades your school teaches and the maximum students you can enroll, among other factors. Once you admit the students who satisfy the admission criteria for each grade, you would need to divide them into 'manageable' groups based on certain factors, and allocate your teachers so that they can manage and teach specific groups of students.

Why do we organize in this manner at all? And what determines the way you would group students and teachers within, and across years? What determines the nature, size, and composition of these groups? How do these groups interact or relate with each other? How do they evolve over time?

## ORGANIZING INTO GROUPS

The grouping could be influenced by curricular and skill development goals – what we expect our children to master before they move on to the next level. It could be our accent or priority on academic research, vocational education, or professional education, shaped by our national growth aspirations. It could also be led by our notions of 'adults' from a psychological development perspective or a workforce/economic perspective or even from the perspective of a system of governance such as democracy (you can vote if you are an adult; you are an adult if you are over 18 years of age). Another important influencing factor is how much education is considered to be a public 'good', and whether it is the government's responsibility to make it available universally. For example, consider the Right to Education in India, a mandate by law for the provision of free and compulsory schooling for children in the age group of 6-14 years, and how it affects our organization of schooling. These factors shape the core organizing principles of grouping in our education systems – they provide the guidelines on why and how we should organize into smaller groups.

Once we have agreed on these organizing principles, we are presented with the problem of designing systems that are aligned with them. We have to design the systems keeping in mind the constraints of the always scarce and expensive resources such as infrastructure and people, and by balancing these constraints with our goals of equity, access, and excellence. For example, it may be efficient for us to have large class sizes, but we may believe that if we did not maintain effective teacher-pupil ratios, it may reduce the quality of instruction and thereby compromise our ultimate goals. We have also to design for manageability. After all, how can we design a system without paying heed to how we shall enforce rules and structures and monitor conformance and performance?

## EDUCRACY

Our solution to these challenges appears to be a very industrial way of doing things, almost like organizing a production line at a factory. Raw material comes in, and it is processed in chunks or groups, and over time transformed through a series of steps into finished products. But the industrial metaphor can only be taken so far. Education researcher Audrey Watters[20] observes that this view of industrialization is inherently ahistorical, because research shows little correlation between the

20 Watters, Audrey (2015, April 25). The invented history of 'the factory model of education', retrieved on December 1, 2017 from http://hackeducation.com/2015/04/25/factory-model

industrial revolution and the evolution of the school system. Our classrooms are not automated machines spewing outputs with a degree of tolerable error. There is chaos and creativity at the level of the individual classroom that cannot be described by the popular industrial and imperialist conception of education.

Our education systems are, instead, modeled on the principles of bureaucracy. This model was articulated by Max Weber,[21] a noted sociologist, who elaborated on a form of organization in which power and control at the one end, and individual independence at the other, are balanced in a rational-legal way. Let us call it an *educracy* - the combination of two terms – education and bureaucracy – signifying the underlying bureaucratic approach to education.

There is a clear separation of roles all the way from the policy maker to the teacher. There is a clear division of labor so that accountability can be placed at the level of the role, and this role is articulated legally. There is compartmentalization by function that is performed at every level (teaching or non-teaching). Knowledge at each role and function level is codified into rulebooks, normed practices, and guidelines. Functions have their own hierarchy of task specialization within the structure. Selection of people is meant to be impersonal and based on technical qualifications. Finally, there is an established chain of command which operates to monitor, implement, and ensure that goals are met and the system works efficiently.

In this context, the debate on how we create and structure groups of students within and across years, and 'administer' education to them, is vitally important. After all, it impacts all our lives fundamentally. The groups that we belonged to at school usually have had a profound impact on our later lives with some long lasting bonds of shared experiences and affinities being created there.

---

21 Mulder, Patty (2017, April 18). Bureaucratic theory by Max Weber, retrieved on November 4, 2017 from https://www.toolshero.com/management/bureaucratic-theory-weber/

## ORGANIZING INTO GROUPS

What are the factors that schools consider when deciding the nature, size, and composition of groups and what choices do they have in a local context? Many schools may not have that choice – they may cater to small catchment areas, and low student enrolments may be the norm. Many others may have to deal with excessive demand and build strict criteria for selection. On the flip side, choices may not be equally available for all parents to make.

In schools, the residential location (catchment area) of the student plays a major role in admissions. It may also be strictly mandated by policy makers. Other factors include the child's age, ability, and past record, parents' background and education, religion, social and economic standing and many other criteria. In countries such as India that have a legal provision for free and compulsory education, there is a mandate for private schools to admit students from the under-privileged and economically weaker sections of society up to 25 percent of their total strength. Some boards of education may be established to serve a specific category of students (such as rural students or open schooling). Reservation of seats (affirmative action) in educational institutions may also be practiced to ensure equitable access to educational opportunities for the under-served or socially deprived communities. Admission is finally limited by the allowed capacity, in terms of infrastructure and staffing, that the school has.

Another factor influencing group formation is that the entry to a grade level is normally contingent on performance in the preceding grade level. India decided to move to a policy where there would be no-detention of students from grades 1-8 by law under the Right to Free and Compulsory Education Act, irrespective of performance, but systemic backlash has prompted a reversal of that provision.[22]

---

22 The Wire (2017, August 3). Union cabinet approves scrapping of no-detention clause in RTE Act, retrieved on November 5, 2017 from https://thewire.in/164159/union-cabinet-no-detention-clause-rte/

Age to grade matching is also not without its problems – in India, nearly 30 million children are either over or underage as per their age-grade levels.[23] This age-grade mismatch has serious impacts on grade-wise progress, grade repetitions and dropouts numbers. It is not just age that matters, many other factors may contribute to students not being at similar levels of proficiency when they exit or pass a grade level and enter another.

To compound the situation, in many cases the educracy may not be entirely able to follow its own rules and designs. For example, in 2015-16, 33.5 percent of all schools in India had enrolments of less than 50 students (which translates to about 0.5 million schools and about 12 million students), a proportion which has increased rapidly from 24.3 percent in 2005. About eight percent of all Indian schools are single teacher schools (which translates to over 100,000 schools). Only about 6.2 percent of these single teacher schools have more than 15 students. The nature and composition of groups in these scenarios is vastly different, and therefore, the rules and designs for such scenarios have to be different.

## SIZING GROUPS

What about class sizes? Do they really matter? An important factor, both from manageability and from a teaching perspective, is the debate on class sizes and what is the optimum group size that is most suitable for teaching and learning.

Small sized groups are preferred for formal instruction because they increase the possibility of personal attention and flexibility in dealing with the curriculum. But smaller groups mean more teachers and more

---

23 6.56 percent or about 8.46 million children at primary level were underage while 5.44 percent or about seven million children in primary were overage. For the upper primary (classes 6-8), 8.3 percent or about 5.6 million children were underage while 11.12 percent or about 7.51 million children were overage. U-DISE Flash Statistics 2015-16, retrieved on April 30, 2019 from http://udise.in/Downloads/Publications/Documents/Flash_Statistics-2015-16_(Elementary).pdf

resources – which translates into more funding for teachers, infrastructure, materials, and training.

Research is divided on the issue of class size. A study[24] that surveyed existing literature on the impact of class size on outcomes suggests that not every school treats this as an important priority. In fact, a thorough review of the scientific evidence shows a startling finding: class size reduction may be one of the least effective educational investments.

The push for lower class sizes has led many countries to aggressively spend on scaling infrastructure and teacher development. But in many countries, the return on investment has been questionable. In India, for example, despite several reforms and investments towards increasing the availability of educational opportunities, the ASER (Annual Status of Education Report) reports show that even minimum levels of learning have not been achieved. Only 20.2 percent of Class III children could do a 2-digit subtraction. Less than half (43.2 percent) of Class III students can read a text of Class I.[25] Just about one in four children in Class III in an average rural school is at "grade" level in reading and in mathematics.[26] The National Achievement Survey (NAS) 2015, reports that only 36 percent of Class V students scored more than 50 percent in reading comprehension and 37 percent scored more than 50 percent in mathematics. All this despite an improving pupil-teacher ratio (PTR) – from 32 in 2008-09 to 24 in 2005-16.[27]

---

24 Hanushek, Eric A (1998). Improving student achievement: is reducing class size the answer?, Policy Brief, Progressive Policy Institute, retrieved on August 13, 2017 from http://hanushek.stanford.edu/sites/default/files/publications/class%20size.ppi6_.revised.pdf

25 ASER (Annual Status of Education Report) 2016 (Rural) findings, retrieved on November 26, 2017 from http://img.asercentre.org/docs/Publications/ASER%20Reports/ASER%202016/Report%20sections/aser2016-nationalfindings.pdf

26 Annual Status of Education Report (Rural) 2016, Provisional, January 18, 2017, retrieved on November 26, 2017 from http://img.asercentre.org/docs/Publications/ASER%20Reports/ASER%202016/aser_2016.pdf

27 NCERT (2015). What students of class V know and can do, A summary of national achievement survey, Class V (Cycle 4), 2015, National Council for Educational Research and Training retrieved on April 30, 2019 from http://www.ncert.nic.in/departments/nie/esd/pdf/NAS_Class_V_(Cycle%204)_Summary_Report_National.pdf

In the USA, PTR fell about 35 percent from about 27:1 to about 17:1 overall between 1950 and 1995 (remember that the USA scaled to maximize its gross enrolment ratio by the late 1990s by building enough infrastructure).[28] However, the National Assessment of Educational Progress (NAEP), USA reports indicate that there was no significant difference in the performance levels of 17-year-olds between 1970 and 1996. According to Hanushek,[29] there isn't any significant correlation between class size and student performance and numerous studies have established that. In fact, looking at the international assessments results, it would seem that American students have relatively under-performed.

At the other extreme end, while some large groups may become unwieldy to administer and control via *educratic* means, other large and diverse groups may benefit from processes and techniques designed for pluralistic thinking and democratic interaction. In the digital space, in higher and professional education, the evidence of the early Massive Open Online Courses (MOOCs) such as CCK08 show that large group interaction can be beneficial if designed properly.[30] In a cMOOC (Connectivist MOOC, the original format of the MOOCs), people form a loose network (open, no membership bar) based on interest, the community members decide to engage on a theme/topic, supply the resources that interest them and those they think will interest others, engage freely on certain ideas, contribute to and document/reflect upon their learning and use interaction tools that they are comfortable with.

All these considerations impact the nature, size, and composition of groups. But how do these groups evolve over time in terms of their nature and composition? Are they always fixed and unchangeable, or

---

28 World Bank (1989). The World Bank Data, retrieved on August 13, 2017 from http://data.worldbank.org/indicator/SE.PRM.ENRR?end=1989&locations=US&start=1971

29 Hanushek, Eric A (1998). Improving student achievement: is reducing class size the answer? Policy Brief, Progressive Policy Institute, retrieved on August 13, 2017 from http://hanushek.stanford.edu/sites/default/files/publications/class%20size.ppi6_.revised.pdf

30 Baxi, Viplav (2015, January 13). Whither Indian MOOCs, retrieved on November 4, 2017 from https://learnos.wordpress.com/2015/01/13/whither-indian-moocs/

do they change, break apart or transform in some way? Is the change a conscious process followed by schools or does it happen naturally?

## THE EVOLUTION OF GROUPS

Schools generally make grouping decisions on a continuous basis across school years based on several reasons such as the number of dropouts or repeaters at a level and the new entrants at that level. It is possible that the group size may increase or decrease, or some groups may be eliminated altogether because of exits or some groups added because of the increases due to new entrants. In general terms, the proportion of schools and enrolments may also decline significantly (as we see in India) as we move across different stages of education – primary to upper primary, secondary, senior secondary higher and tertiary education – often not proportionately leading to changes in the PTR across school years.

Schools may reorganize students for social reasons as well, ostensibly for them to benefit from coming into contact with students in other groups, gain academically and not get too comfortable with just one set of peers.

> 'We do not want children to settle into groups since class X is a crucial class and we want students of different capabilities to be spread homogenously across sections. But we are mindful of the challenges it poses and make exceptions when there is a genuine reason. For instance, we do not separate identical twins,' says Revathy Bonns, Principal, Madras Christian College Matriculation Higher Secondary School.[31]

Schools may also reorganize students into groups depending upon their abilities or special needs. High-ability groups or sub-groups may get

31 Sridhar, Asha (2016, July 12). Good, bad or better: the student shuffling saga, *The Hindu*, retrieved on August 13, 2017 from http://www.thehindu.com/features/education/school/good-bad-or-better-the-student-shuffling-saga/article3595542.ece

specialized attention, better resources and more focus on preparation for standardized tests and college entrance examinations.

Another way of reorganization is tracking – the separation of students by stream of studies or vocations. It is possible that schools may use ability in a stream as a criterion for reorganization or they may place students in certain vocational streams, sometimes with a bias that not every student 'needed' or wanted to make it to college for further academic studies.

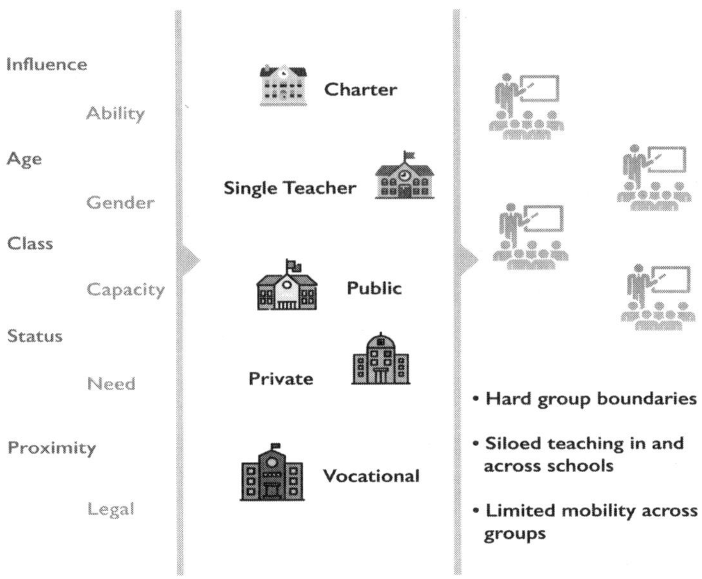


**Figure 5: Homogenizing the diversity in students through groups and schools**

These reorganizations change group dynamics and the interpersonal dynamics of its members, the effects of which are not exactly determinate. For example, did the modified spread of students of different capabilities across sections cause improvement of the average student performance in the Madras school mentioned above? Or did it raise significant socialization issues?

Of related importance is to understand how the parents' groups reorganize to accompany the reorganization of student groups. Given the fact that parents play an important role in the process, we do need to consider the impact the reorganization has on their networks and the level of trust they need to build each year with new peer parents. Since an important part of their interaction with other parents is around the teaching-learning in class, the breaking of old bonds and creation of new ones around the new configurations can introduce real discontinuities that can impact both student socialization and progress.

Assessments effectively become the most important tools for making these decisions of progression across years, and reorganization of students across various groups in different years. Pathways through the school and college years are determined by how students perform, and both entry and exit points are signified by these assessments. It is however important here to emphasize that the quality of assessments, like the quality of teaching and learning, needs to be very reliable in order to make the right progression and reorganization decisions, and be based on the right competency frameworks.

Of real importance to our claim of child centered education, is the concept of student choice. The choice as to which group to belong is largely outside the reach of students. It is heavily influenced by peer and parental pressure. This eases up slightly in higher classes with more subject, institutional, and stream choices, or perhaps for high performers. But for the most part, the reorganization is out of the realm of student control, a fate they have to accept.

Once organized in a particular way, how do these groups interact with each other? Are the group boundaries porous and open to exchange and flow of ideas, and interactions? How segmented is the activity in one group from the activities in other groups? How does this impact student progress and opportunities?

## GROUPING CREATES BOUNDARIES

What is really interesting is that once these groups are formed, their boundaries limit their opportunities for interaction. Group boundaries are not very porous when it comes to either teaching or learning. Apart from certain whole-grade activities, which tend to be largely co-curricular in nature rather than academic, students in one group have little or no opportunity to learn from students in other groups.

Since different teachers take responsibility for different groups, it is highly unlikely that teaching styles, content or activities of teaching and learning will be uniform across groups. Teachers may coordinate the progress through curricula in a grade and create mechanisms for collectively synchronizing activities, but the environment for learning within each group may be drastically different. Within these reorganizations, the teacher's role in bringing the group together to create a rich environment of caring and sharing between students becomes really important. Collaboration can positively impact the performance of a group. A shared sense of purpose can help bind the group into alignment with the teacher's objectives. Students working together can increase the efficacy of teachers immensely. Nowhere is this better illustrated than in stories like 'To Sir, with Love', the famous movie, 'Dead Poets Society' and, of course, in group activities such as sports and performing arts.

Groups with more effective teachers, higher trust, and more engaging activities, will likely be at an advantage compared to groups without them. The level of collaboration, shared reflection, and adaption of teaching will depend heavily on both the school's own emphasis on excellence and commitment to teaching outcomes, and on an individual teacher's commitment to her own continuous learning.

There is the administrative dimension of maintaining multiple groups that needs to be considered as well. Every group has to have a teacher-manager, who is responsible for managing the group, interacting with parents, planning group activities, handling individual issues, tracking attendance, and reporting progress, apart from her duties as a subject teacher. Multiple groups have to be tracked and managed separately, requiring a whole-grade level coordination of teaching and learning activities, progress tracking and reporting.

The task of dividing into cohesive and manageable groups is an important and complex one for the school bureaucracy. But does it really work well in practice?

India represents an interesting case study of complexity, with wide diversity at scale.[32] As per the 2015-16 Unified District Information of School Education (U-DISE, under the Ministry of Human Resource Development) estimates, India has about 129 million children enrolled in classes 1-5, 67.59 million in classes 6-8, for a total of 196.71 million in classes 1-8 (ages 6-14). It has nearly 1.5 million schools spread across 680 districts (administrative units).

Let us keep in mind this scale that the Indian bureaucracy has to contend with. Just the number of single teacher schools in India would be greater than all the public schools combined in the USA (around 98 thousand in 2013-14).[33]

The Indian bureaucracy has to therefore, contend with great complexity in the nature and composition of groups containing students of diverse backgrounds and abilities, the evolution of groups and the interaction within and between these groups.

This is a real challenge. Bureaucracies establish standardization and attempt to drive predictability – a homogeneity of structures and practices. When faced with diversity, a bureaucracy practices a 'controlled

32 U-DISE Flash Statistics 2015-16, retrieved on April 30, 2019 from http://udise.in/Downloads/Publications/Documents/Flash_Statistics-2015-16_(Elementary).pdf

33 National Center for Educational Statistics, USA, retrieved on November 4, 2017 from https://nces.ed.gov/fastfacts/display.asp?id=84

homogeneity' – it allows individual variations in structures and practices, but limits the variation itself.

## MANAGING GROUPS

In India, a national level education policy on education acts as a guideline for various boards of education at the national and state levels.[34] There is an advisory body called the CABE (Central Advisory Board of Education) that advises on the alignment of boards to the education policy guidelines. National and State boards of education (also some autonomous boards), in a cooperative federal structure, take on the responsibilities for managing large numbers of schools. The boards are essentially responsible for managing quality, conducting entrance and exit (clearing) examinations and inducting and regulating affiliated schools. Many other countries follow a similar approach.

There is diversity in the types of schools according to the type of audience they serve. The Charter schools in the USA that are focused on low-income and minority groups, or the Jawahar Navodaya Vidyalayas in India that are focused on rural talent, are examples. Canadian public school boards have also set up different schools based on different interests.[35] Open schools follow a different system and cater to needs of students who cannot attend regular school. There are niche private schools that are affiliated to national or international boards of education or public schools as well as publicly controlled and operated local state or district schools. All these different types of schools are governed by norms, through which the bureaucracy attempts to achieve consistency of outcomes. While norms may be prescribed by the bureaucracy, as we have seen, they are by no means uniformly implementable given the sheer diversity.

34 India has 49 boards of education – from national boards like the CBSE, to individual state boards and even autonomous boards. The government controls the activities of the state and national level boards and regulates the autonomous boards. A voluntary association of various boards called the Council of Boards of School Education in India helps in inter-board coordination and sharing of practices.

35 Downes, Stephen (2008, March 1). Options and opportunities, retrieved on December 18, 2017 from http://www.downes.ca/post/44259

One could argue that the bureaucracy effectively handles these scenarios through teacher training, appropriate pedagogical techniques and efficient segmentation into groups. But consider this. Between 37 and 44 percent of students from class 1-8 in India get less than 60 percent scores in their exams.[36] This means that the teachers have to contend with two out of every five students in every group on average, who are at a distinctly lower level of accomplishment in what they have learnt in the previous year. The norms around grouping are suspect and whatever be the group composition algorithm, it is quite likely that teachers will have to 'teach to the middle' – marginalizing students at the extreme ends of the spectrum.[37] This indicates that the system has not been able to achieve what it was designed to.

## CHANGING THE PARADIGM

What if we tweak this element in the system – change how groups are created and organized? One of the possibilities is to break down the divisions within a grade. Open Schooling accomplishes this to some extent. Provided a student meets entry criteria, she can have more choice and control on how she learns, when and with whom. MOOCs offer a similar mechanism – you can be part of a massive worldwide online network of fellow students.

In schools, an approach could be to get some of the best teachers from within or outside the school to explain concepts for more than one group of students, and allow students to choose the sessions they need to attend to fulfill a learning goal or to satisfy their curiosity. In this case, other teachers could lead interest-based groups providing counseling, hands-on support, and curricular guidance.

---

36 U-DISE Flash Statistics 2015-16, retrieved on April 30, 2019 from http://udise.in/Downloads/Publications/Documents/Flash_Statistics-2015-16_(Elementary).pdf

37 There may, though, be focused strategies for this division, such as ability driven grouping or special needs grouping.

Another mechanism is cooperative learning. Rather than thinking of classes and sections as defined in the traditional schools, cooperative schools are based on team organization and processes. The team organization is present in every aspect of the school, from the classroom to the teachers to the administration of the school. In cooperative learning, students are organized into smaller groups. Interaction within and between the teams forms the basis of learning. Teams work cooperatively to amplify, refine, and extend each other's thinking and knowledge.

Central to the team organization model is ability of teachers to understand and continuously improve on cooperation methods, in a meta-cognitive manner. It is a collegial system where small teams of teachers work together to increase their expertise in cooperative learning, a refreshing change from the traditional systems where there is little or no corresponding pressure on teachers to organize and reflect on their cooperative endeavors even while expecting students to cooperate in controlled situations. Teachers cooperate in various areas – design, plan, co-teaching, and techniques for enhancing cooperation – in a rigorous and disciplined manner. Teachers are organized into vertical teams such that same groups of students are handled through the years by same teacher team, implying greater accountability and shared purpose for learning outcomes. Assessment of their own progress is devised and adapted by the teachers themselves. The curriculum is integrated and themed.

By bringing in the role of the team as the basis of organization, rather than creating silos within which teachers and students operate, cooperative learning structures can positively impact learning outcomes.

> “ When teachers are seen as interchangeable parts in a machine created to mass-produce educated students, they tend to become isolated and alienated from each other and from their work. A congruent organizational structure - one that promotes cooperation at all levels - ensures quality education.[38]

---

38 Johnson, David, W, Roger, T. Johnson, and Edythe Johnson Holubec (1994). ***The cooperative school, new circles of learning***, Chapter 10, Association for Supervision and Curriculum Development, retrieved on November 23, 2017 from http://www.ascd.org/publications/books/194034/chapters/The-Cooperative-School.aspx

These ideas have deep implications of change on many other aspects of our organization of the education system. If we can align the nature, composition, and size of groups in a more personalized and effective manner, if we can structure the evolution pathways of each group according to abilities and interests, and if we can fundamentally alter the way groups interact with each other by systematically breaking down silos, then perhaps we can bring about wide-scale change for the better in the prevailing conventional system.

# #3

# What*If*

**we removed the boundaries between subjects?**

# #3 WHAT *IF* WE REMOVED THE BOUNDARIES BETWEEN SUBJECTS?

*Today we study each subject as a separate discipline. The knowledge, approaches, and processes of learning and teaching are also segmented by subject. Teachers are separated by departments. Progress is also measured per subject. What if we broke these boundaries between subjects? What if we instead had only topics or themes that ran across more than one subject?*

*What if the syllabus was not divided into chapters and topics? What if we built out a curriculum that relied on cross-disciplinary projects needing similar expertise and skills to be developed? What if we allowed students and teachers to contribute to creating their own curriculum rather than mandating it to them? What if we allowed the curriculum to have a life of its own, growing in directions propelled by both academic objectives and interest? What if we shifted our focus from learning to 'know' to learning to 'be'?*

Imagine you are in 385 BCE. Plato has just established the Academy. He believes that true knowledge cannot come from teaching, but from questioning. This 'Socratic' method has become the mainstay of his educational philosophy. Children enter the Academy at the age of six and learn reading, writing, and counting. They focus on literature and poetry, mathematics, history, and science, through storytelling and games. Music and arts are compulsory and so are exercise and discipline. At 20, if students pass the examination, they are taught arithmetic, astronomy, geometry and dialectics, apart from the physical and mathematical sciences. At 30, post another exam, they are required to spend five more years in advanced education on dialectics. If they pass that stage, they are to practice dialectics for 15 years till they can reasonably prove themselves ready to govern their country. The ones who cannot clear any of the exams can take to the professions, or join the administrative or military services.[39]

The subjects to be taught then were determined by both the level of knowledge specialization, and the local social, military, religious and cultural contexts of that time. Even as late as the 18th century, formal and classical education was restricted to few people, and mass education had not yet taken root. As a consequence only a select few were to be taught the arts, language, and philosophy and those that were, would do so in preparation for future roles of leadership, governance and power.

Obviously, the subjects and their depths in 385 BCE and the modern day are very different. Subject areas have become increasingly specialized. New subjects have emerged that had no counterparts in earlier times. Most subjects have gained a corpus sufficient to extend across a student's academic lifetime and beyond. Knowledge is now a large, deep, and complex web exhibiting both vertical specialization and horizontal integration.

---

39 Plato's theory of education, retrieved on April 30, 2019 from http://www.yourarticlelibrary.com/education/platos-theory-of-education/40135

But we have created a curriculum that is segmented into multiple subjects with rather fixed boundaries between them. Is that really a good thing? Do we need more integrated approaches to curricular design? How do we balance between the required vertical (intra-disciplinary) depth and horizontal (cross-disciplinary) breadth?

## BREAKING THE SUBJECT SILOS

Today, teachers are educated on how to effectively 'transmit' these segmented corpora of knowledge to their students using various classroom techniques. The syllabus continues to expand aggressively. New knowledge is being added continuously, and older knowledge is getting more and more compressed within the limitations that the space, weight, and size of textbooks allow. In the present day, we expect students to achieve mastery over the contents of at least five to seven subjects at each grade level.

Educators recognize the importance of bridging different subjects via an integrated curriculum.[40] These integrations have the power to make learning more meaningful, experiential, and engaging. They build 21st century skills such as critical and creative thinking, and social and inter-personal skills, which are important to negotiate the fast changing world. The ability to visualize the connections between concepts across different disciplines provides learners the whole-system perspective. Participating in inquiry and problem-solving, allows learners to construct explanations for their own realities. For example, the scientific understanding of the construction of a devastating atomic bomb has its intra-disciplinary depth, but a corresponding understanding of the ethics, history, and politics of its conception and use should not be ignored.

Teaching techniques and the role of the teacher in the classroom are significantly impacted when using an integrated approach. From being

40 Mathison, Sandra and Melissa Freeman (1997). *The logic of interdisciplinary students*, National Research Center on English Learning and Achievement, retrieved on December 13, 2017 from http://www.albany.edu/cela/reports/mathisonlogic12004.pdf

the 'sage on the stage', the teacher actually becomes the 'guide by the side'. Learners move from being receptacles of knowledge to active agents shaping their own learning.

But teachers may argue that there simply isn't time to do justice to both a vast syllabus for each subject, and to spend quality time in cross-disciplinary connection-making. In this scenario, enabling an integrated (designed) or integrative (constructed by learners and teachers) view to emerge in the traditional, segmented classroom may become very difficult.

The more common method in these traditional settings may be to 'add-on' content and activities that 'connect' to related subjects. This could take the form of additional curricular elements such as projects, real-life applications, special call-outs in textbooks, and value added questions for reflection that promote collaboration, social awareness, critical and creative thinking. But this incremental approach is still driven by the in-place curriculum for each subject. This makes it a supplementary but not a truly integrated approach.[41] This approach does not give learners initiative and control over what they want to learn, does not allow them to breach curriculum boundaries from the very beginning, and continues to consider the teacher at the core (responsible for achieving learning outcomes for a subject) of knowledge dissemination rather than as a facilitator of the learning process (encouraging connection-making in an integrated manner).

If we were to depart from the traditional model, the contrasting approach would be to really build out truly integrated or synergistic curricula – an approach being advocated since the early 1900s by eminent thinkers such as John Dewey.

---

41 Fraser, Deborah (2000). *Curriculum integration: what it is and is not*, Chapter 2, NZCER press, retrieved on April 30, 2019 from http://www.nzcer.org.nz/system/files/press/abstracts/Chapter%202.pdf

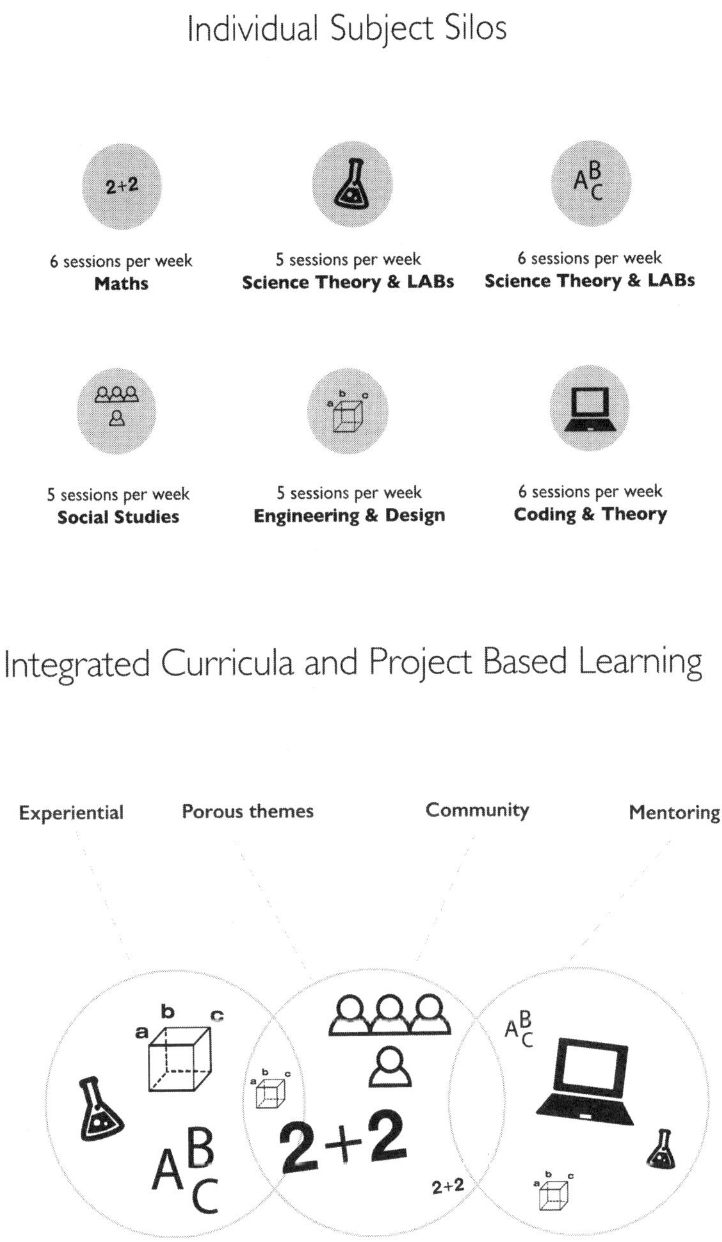


**Figure 6: Individual Subject Silos vs. Integrated Curricula**

> We live in a world where all sides are bound together. All studies grow out of relations in the one great common world. When the child lives in varied but concrete and active relationship to this common world, his studies are naturally unified.[42]

An integrated curriculum approach focuses on themes and real world problems rather than subjects, critical and creative thinking skills rather than rote, cooperation rather than isolation, more student autonomy, and a culture of connection-making rather than imposition of a fixed design.

This is a contrasting approach for many reasons. The school structure is built to impart compartmentalized knowledge in a didactic fashion over short periods of time, while the integrated approach needs much more time and freedom to make the connections. The existing departmental structure creates isolation between teachers, while the contrasting approach expects departmental silos to be greatly diminished. At present, teachers direct the learning while in the contrasting approach, teachers shift towards more personal reflection and learning, becoming reflective guides to students and facilitating the open exchange of ideas. This integrated approach may also require more administrative flexibility and financial support than the traditional system. It definitely impacts our design of content, scheduling and student grouping mechanisms.

Based on research on integrated curricula, a study[43] reveals some of the common components of this approach.

> These definitions support the view that integrated curriculum is an educational approach that prepares children for lifelong learning. There is a strong belief among those who support curriculum integration that schools must look at education as a process for developing abilities

42 Dewey, John (1907). *School and society*, University of Chicago Press, retrieved on December 13, 2017 from https://brocku.ca/MeadProject/Dewey/Dewey_1907/Dewey_1907c.html

43 Lake, Kathy (1994). Integrated curriculum, *School Improvement Research Series*, Education Northwest, retrieved on August 27, 2017 from http://educationnorthwest.org/sites/default/files/integrated-curriculum.pdf

required by life in the twenty-first century, rather than discrete, departmentalized subject matter.

Integrated or inter-disciplinary curricula rely on a combination of subjects, focus on projects, moving beyond textbooks, and emphasizing the relationships among concepts. By allowing theme-based units and flexible schedules and student groupings, integrated curricula help build essential 21st century skills.

## THE PROJECT BASED LEARNING APPROACH

Of particular interest is the project based learning (PBL) method for organizing curriculum. PBL eschews the traditional division into subjects. Instead the progression from year to year is marked by successful completion of a number of projects. So, instead of giving credits or marks on a per subject basis, students are awarded credits or scores based on inter-disciplinary and thematic projects. Each project demands that the student or student group research all aspects of the topic – the subject/domain, the real world contexts, the choice of research method, interaction with experts and communities, feedback from peers - at varying levels of complexity. It necessarily builds reflective capabilities, and prepares students to become better, more responsive communicators and collaborators.

Let us take the example of the PBL curriculum at the Minnesota New Country School (MNCS), USA. At MNCS, students get credits based on the projects they undertake.[44] The number of projects (and thereby credits) required to be created and their complexity differs from grade to grade. Projects follow given structures, guidelines, and processes from approval to final presentation and are closely monitored. For example, a grade seven project must have pre-approval by a proposal team, finalization prior to a five-minute presentation, documentation on hours of effort and resources utilized and a practiced presentation. A

44 MNCS Handbook, retrieved on November 20, 2017 from https://newcountryschool.files.wordpress.com/2016/08/mncs-parent-student-handbook-2017-2018.pdf

grade nine project includes all that plus the use of real world resources/situations, creative problem solving, and cross-curriculum exploration with in-depth research. In the 10th grade, a student would have to complete a project that has a detailed proposal with a plan, a project rubric that is approved by the sophomore team, career exploration and planning, a project that accounts for 1+ credits, a 10-minute rehearsed and approved presentation, a three-page research paper and interaction with a community expert resource.

> Graduation requirements include completion of 70 credits, completion of all Minnesota Academic Standards,[45] completion of tests like the ACT test,[46] and the completion of a Senior Project. The Senior Project is quite complex. Students must show at least 300 hours of documented academic work, display a significant amount of creativity or 'brain strain', make a 25-minute presentation to the public and write a high quality research paper (minimum 10 pages).

## MODELING THE INTEGRATED CURRICULUM

Some researchers have divided the approaches to integrated curriculum into three broad categories[47] - multidisciplinary (theme-based), intra-disciplinary (within subject linkages) and fusion (when skills, knowledge, and attitudes are 'fused' into the curriculum). Robin Fogarty presents ten different models[48] of curriculum integration:

> Beginning with an exploration within single discipline (the fragmented, connected, and nested models), and continuing with models that

45 Minnesota State Academic Standards, retrieved on April 30, 2019 from http://education.state.mn.us/MDE/fam/stds/

46 ACT Test, retrieved on November 20, 2017 from http://www.act.org/content/act/en/products-and-services/the-act.html

47 Drake, Susan M, and Rebecca C. Burns (2011). Meeting standards through integrated curriculum, Association for Supervision and Curriculum Development, retrieved on April 30, 2019 from http://www.ascd.org/publications/books/103011/chapters/What-Is-Integrated-Curriculum%C2%A2.aspx

48 Fogarty, Robin (1991). Ten ways to integrate curriculum, Association for Supervision and Curriculum Development, retrieved on April 30, 2019 from https://pdfs.semanticscholar.org/fc84/06745befdf07ad521450d7434df379c72c48.pdf

> integrate across several disciplines (the sequenced, shared, webbed, threaded, and integrated models), the continuum ends with models that operate within learners themselves (the immersed model) and finally across networks of learners (the networked model).

The fragmented model, which is the traditional model, sees each subject as its own entity. The connected model makes the intra-disciplinary linkages explicit. The nested model combines related concepts, giving each lesson a multi-dimensional aspect. In the sequenced model, the units and concepts being taught are arranged in tandem with related topics across subjects being sequenced in a purposeful manner. The shared model is where two disciplines may be taught together using a single frame and overlapping concepts, just like in a binocular view. The webbed model integrates all disciplines within an organizing theme, in a cross-disciplinary manner. The threaded model is all about meta-curriculum, focusing on top skills (such as thinking skills) rather than focusing on individual subjects. The Integrated model is like the shared model, but runs in a cross-disciplinary format with all major disciplines connected to each other, like in a kaleidoscopic view. In the immersed model, integration occurs within learners, as an interest and focus based activity. In the networked model, multiple dimensions and directions of focus with the learners direct the integration itself. These models propose different ways in which content, instruction and learning are organized in an integrated approach.

STEM (Science, Technology, Engineering and Mathematics) education follows an integrated approach by definition. STEM educators understand that they have to give much more emphasis to the problem or theme upfront rather than diving into any one subject directly and making the connections from within it. The themes they select are therefore, much more aligned to wider real world problems or experiences, rather than narrow and abstract subject lines.

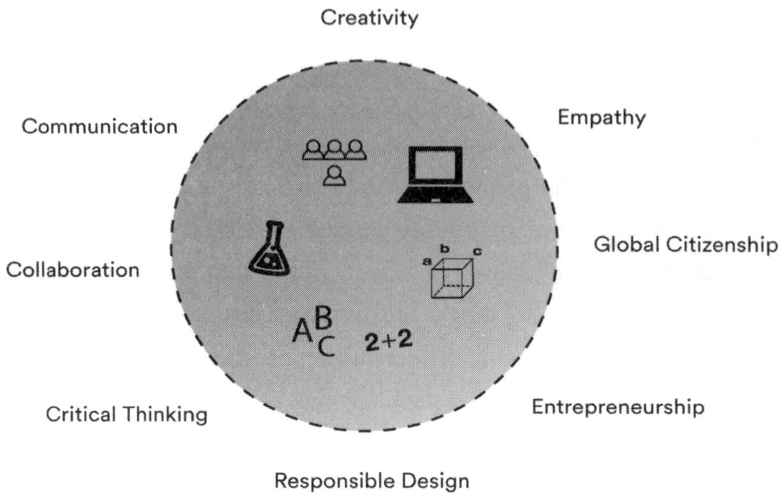


**Figure 7: Components of STEAM education**

Proponents of STEM education also recognize the role performing arts can play in enhancing the quality of integrated curricula. Arts is considered an integral part of STEM education, so much so that STEM education is interchangeably called STEAM (with the 'A' standing for Arts) education. By including Arts in STEM education, the positive impact of participation in Arts on students' achievements and capabilities comes into focus.[49]

> Learning is deepest when learners have the capacity to represent what they have learned, and the multiple disciplines of the arts all provide modes of representation.
>
> … (a study of) 25,000 (secondary school American) students (over 10 years) demonstrates that students with high levels of arts participation outperform "arts-poor" students by virtually every measure.

49 Fiske, Edward B. (ed). ***Champions of change, the impact of the arts on learning***, Artsedge, The Kennedy Center, retrieved on August 27, 2017 from http://artsedge.kennedy-center.org/champions/pdfs/champsreport.pdf

The role of performing arts including theatre, music, and dance is emphasized as a way to encourage a greater depth of exploration and representation, demonstration of a wider span of skills and deeper engagement with the learning process. Studies show that students who participate in performing arts based activities, display much greater connection with their communities, are more engaged and motivated to learn, and exhibit greater positive behaviors and attitudes towards their school and the society.

Arts in STEAM is considered more broadly to include both Arts and Humanities subjects such as languages, literature, art, religion, law, psychology, sociology, economics and philosophy. Real-life experiential STEAM projects could include a healthy dose of the Arts, which are as important as the natural sciences, mathematics and technology aspects of the projects. This inclusion creates the awareness of how important design is, and how innovation needs to be contextualized to local social and environmental contexts. No part of STEAM based learning is seen independent of hands-on creation or 'making'. The recent spurt of interest in *Makerspaces* complements integrated approaches. *Makerspaces* are both physical and virtual spaces for creation. They could be physically constructed lab spaces where students could come in and use tools and materials to construct things in the arts, technology, engineering, robotics and other fields. They could also manifest in the form of online or blended communities of practice around certain themes that could scaffold early learners and provide them a space for experimentation and exploration.

The integrated approach also requires that both teachers and students incorporate new approaches to teaching and learning,[50] new behaviors and thinking practices. They would need a fair amount of training and acclimatization on this. They would also need to have a fair idea of how

50 Contardi Gina, Michelle Fall, Gina Flora, Jodi Gandee and Carrie Treadway (2000). Integrated curriculum, a group investigation project, EDP 603, retrieved on August 26, 2017 from http://www.users.miamioh.edu/shermalw/edp603_group3-f00.html

their subjects overlap with others, and even gain some proficiency in others they would not normally have encountered in a traditional segmented curriculum.

Assessments would also change to include more emphasis on areas such as solving real world problems using skills such as reflection, reasoning and deduction. There would be consequent changes in the measurement and evaluation of skills (evidence centered assessment), that would also place further demands on the teacher to embrace many non-traditional testing methods.

One of the significant outcomes of the integrated approach that it encourages teachers to achieve a greater degree of collaboration with their peers, integrating across subject and level boundaries. It encourages teachers to share some of their autonomy and control over their own classroom activities, by co-creating and co-assessing performance on student activities with their peers.

This naturally implies a lot of teamwork and meta-cognitive reflection between teachers, and their reliance on a wider network of coaches and experts on an ongoing basis. In fact, the wider network can include professionals, community leaders, experts and many other stakeholders, whose collective contribution to a child's development can be very significant. With an aim to make children reflective practitioners of what they learn, teachers can help them learn to *be*, rather than just learn to *know* or *do*.

Apart from the challenges of design, there are challenges in execution as well.[51] We need to provide evidence of how teachers actually engage students in the classroom in an integrated approach. Teachers need to span subject silos and departmental boundaries. The design of activities needs to incorporate inter-disciplinary connection making. Competency

---

51 Baxi, Viplav (2015, March 13). CBSE open text based assessments – lip service or silver bullet, ***Viplav Baxi's Meanderings***, retrieved on April 30, 2019 from https://learnos.wordpress.com/2015/03/13/otba/

frameworks need to be designed to account for the complexity in integrated curricula such that assessments are meaningful and reliable. Teacher professional development and certification criteria need to be redesigned, perhaps using some of the different integration models themselves.

The blurring of boundaries in this way impacts quite radically the existing way of transacting curriculum and fostering 21st century skills. But it has also been found to positively impact learners and teachers. What if we did evolve to alternative curricular systems that respected this? Can we make experience rather than compact knowledge the center of the curriculum? Can we bring to learners greater control of their curriculum?

# #4

# What*If*

teachers spent dedicated time every day on sharing notes on classroom experiences?

# #4 WHAT*IF* TEACHERS SPENT DEDICATED TIME EVERY DAY ON SHARING NOTES ON CLASSROOM EXPERIENCES?

*Teaching is a challenging job. It is complex to teach in a diverse environment with the many constraints and challenges that teachers face every day. In this context, it is extremely important for teachers to find ways to grow professionally and enhance their impact on their students.*

*How do teachers improve with every teaching experience? How do they share their growth with others? How do they invite and contribute to critique? Do they reflect enough on how they are teaching? What if that sharing was open? What if networks and communities of teachers amplified what works and how it works? What if teachers dedicated time to learning about how they teach and how they learn? What if teachers could learn through communities of practice rather than top down training programs?*

If you are a teacher, you have surely been already confronted with a wide range of challenges in your classrooms. You may have had issues such as managing class discipline, handling 'difficult' students, keeping pace with the syllabus, innovating to find new ways of generating interest in your class, managing regular assessment tasks, and perhaps even coping with technology or new knowledge and experiences of your students. You are probably not alone, and you may be able to reach out for help from peers and experts. New problems surface continuously and you are under pressure to innovate and extend your own knowledge so that you are better able to cope with them. Traditional training happens episodically and may not be tailored to your exact unique needs. You have precious little time for your own reflection. How do you learn more about your subject, classroom techniques you could adopt or improve on, leadership, problem solving and the effective use of technology? Who do you learn from? How do you keep motivated to do more?

The way the school is organized, in general, it is geared towards students learning from teachers, but not so much about teachers reflecting on their own learning and teaching, and learning from and contributing to the growth of other teachers on a continuous basis. Schools do not consistently allocate dedicated time and space every day on this subject, just like they would do for the subjects children learn. Many schools do conduct teacher training, some possibly encourage joint teacher projects, and in some schools, teachers do take the initiative to develop themselves professionally. But the large part of a teacher's teaching life is filled with things other than reflection and collaborative learning. This is not to suggest that these do not happen in formal or informal ways already. The idea is to put more focus on them as part of an analysis of teachers' time, especially when it comes to establishing a consistent pattern for a teacher's own learning and development, within the context of the wider community of teachers that they belong to.

## TIME AND TEACHING

How do teachers spend their time? One study by OECD[52] shows the variation across countries in teaching time. The study separates teaching time (direct instruction in class) from non-teaching time (preparing lesson plans, correction, in-service meetings and staff meetings). For pre-primary, the total working days range from 144 to 251 across the countries surveyed, while the actual teaching time ranges from about 500 to 1300 hours. On an average this is about 1044 hours per year at the Pre-Primary level. For primary schools the average is 784 hours per year; for lower secondary it is an average of 703 hours, while for upper secondary it is 657 hours. Primary teachers teach an average of 4.3 hours a day. Interestingly, the average hours spent teaching reduces from pre-primary to upper secondary.

What is especially interesting is how teachers spend their 'non-teaching time'. The tasks for a sample of the lower secondary teachers, in order of most time spent, seem to be lesson preparation, corrections, administrative tasks, team work, counseling and then other tasks. Less than 10 percent of the total hours in the week is on team work (assuming zero overlap between tasks). Country and education board specific policies also impact changes in the breakup of teaching and non-teaching hours and time. The proportion of such non-teaching time ranges from 19% (pre-primary), to 34% (primary), 40% (lower secondary) and 42% (upper secondary) for the countries in the study.

Another group of studies[53] estimated that in the USA, teachers spend 50 percent of their time on instruction, 20 percent on lesson

---

52 OECD (2018). Indicator D4: How much time do teachers spend teaching?, in Education at a Glance 2018: OECD Indicators, OECD Publishing, retrieved on November 4, 2018 from https://www.oecd-ilibrary.org/indicator-d4-how-much-time-do-teachers-spend-teaching_5j8lgv9zswxx.pdf?itemId=%2Fcontent%2Fcomponent%2Feag-2018-31-en&mimeType=pdf

53 Rasmussen, Darin (2016, March 31). Breaking down a teachers' day: A close look at how the hours are spent, *Edmentum*, retrieved on September 2, 2017 from http://blog.edmentum.com/breaking-down-teachers%E2%80%99-day-close-look-how-hours-are-spent

preparation, 10 percent on test preparation and less than three percent on professional development. Given a total of 1950 hours, this translates to about 1000 hours of direct instruction and less than 60 hours of time on professional development in an entire year.[54]

In another survey, on Washington public school teachers,[55] it was found that teachers spent 1.4 hours additionally over and above their contracted time every day. 72.9 percent of teachers' time was spent in direct instruction, 15-17.8 percent of time was spent in getting students prepared for the standardized testing, and about 27.2 percent was spent in communications with parents, professional development, participation in learning communities, and other tasks.

In yet another study sponsored by the Bill and Melinda Gates foundation,[56] collaboration with other teachers was estimated to be a 15-minute activity out of an over seven-hour work day, on an average. In contrast, the five winners of The New Teacher Project (TNTP) Fishman Prize 2015 for superlative classroom practice found that they spend less than 50 percent of their time in direct instruction[57] and the majority of the rest on planning, curriculum design, coaching and mentoring activities.

These studies show that there is a variation in the amount of time that is spent in non-teaching activities and that direct instruction constitutes a large part of how teachers usually spend their time. In the non-teaching

---

54 If we assume that 80 percent of that instruction is whole-class, and the average class size is (say) 25 students, this translates into 200 hours of individualized instruction/attention or about eight hours per student per year (or roughly 15 minutes a week). Parents get much lesser time than that, obviously. Generally speaking, it points to extremely little time spent with parents or students, which should prompt serious concern. It gets worse with larger class sizes and multi-grade classrooms.

55 CWU Teacher Time Study: How Washington Public School Teachers Spend Their Work Days, retrieved on April 30, 2019 from https://www.cwu.edu/sites/default/files/images/teachertimestudy.pdf

56 Primary Sources: 2012, America's teachers on the teaching profession, A project of Scholastic and the Bill & Melinda Gates Foundation, p 14, retrieved on September 2, 2017 from https://www.scholastic.com/primarysources/pdfs/Gates2012_full.pdf

57 This is how some of America's best teachers spend their time, retrieved on April 30, 2019 from https://brightthemag.com/this-is-how-some-of-america-s-best-teachers-spend-their-time-4a0ded0fbb56

time, it is also clear that very little time is actually spent on professional development or reflective activities.

In some countries, such as India, the problems are complicated by other factors. Absenteeism of teachers, too many administrative and training tasks, poor working conditions, inimical pay, lack of adequate professional support, large numbers of vacancies, overloaded work days, pressures of multi-grade classrooms and other such factors, give even less time for teachers to develop themselves professionally or to collaborate with others. Motivation in such circumstances is also low. Many teachers are forced to pursue other employment opportunities post-school hours due to financial pressures and this further reduces the opportunity for any self-development to happen. Low self-esteem and lack of social respect are two other factors that affect self-development. The problems are compounded for ad-hoc teachers (temporary staff) as they are even more deprived of the opportunities for training and development. The PROBE report from India highlights these and many more issues:[58]

> Most importantly, it is hard to think of a more damning indictment of the education system than this single fact: teachers do not even conceive of their work in terms of creating an environment where all children can learn. They continue to teach the way they were taught, in the absence of a space for questioning, analysis and reconstruction.

Are outcomes better achieved when teachers spend more of their time in lesson preparation or in carving out disciplined time for their own professional development and for structured collaboration with other teachers? How does collaboration and professional development look like in multi-grade classrooms and single teacher schools? Taking a step back, are there other critical factors we need to resolve before we can even talk about professional development and collaboration?

58 PROBE revisited, A report on elementary education in India, Oxford University Press, p17, retrieved on August 4, 2018 from https://www.researchgate.net/publication/227467201_Probe_Revisited_A_Report_on_Elementary_Education_in_India

## APPROACHES TO PROFESSIONAL DEVELOPMENT

The fact is that professional development will depend on specific circumstances and it will vary from self-led evolutionary approaches to top down mandated approaches. There may not be a single true answer or solution.

From a practice perspective, viewed from an 'administrator' top-down lens, this takes the shape of mandatory and optional training and certifications, often linked to career progression. The design of the programs could be offline, online or blended. It could be episodic or continuous professional development. Education boards or schools themselves would perhaps organize many of these developmental opportunities for teachers, but some percentage of these opportunities could come from online or other courses and certifications. The scope of these formal training events may be driven by design decisions taken at top levels – for example, moving from episodic term end exams to continuous evaluation through the year. But they are not necessarily personalized to the teacher's specific needs, thus presenting an important challenge that needs to be resolved. Learning by teachers could be more useful if it was thought as informal rather than formal. Informal Learning, a term coined by Jay Cross (who also coined the term 'eLearning'), is the everyday learning, 'which enables you to participate successfully in life, at work, and in the groups that matter to you. Informal learning is the unofficial, unscheduled, impromptu way people learn to do their jobs.'[59]

Cross believed that professional learning followed a 70:20:10 principle – 10 percent formal learning, 20 percent coaching and mentoring and 70 percent informally on-the-job and through social conversations. He brought out the relevance of networks in our daily professional learning.

---

59 Malamed, Connie (2010, February). Informal learning: An interview with Jay Cross, www.theelearningcoach.com, retrieved on December 14, 2017 from http://theelearningcoach.com/elearning2-0/informal-learning-an-interview-with-jay-cross/

Teacher professional development should also be viewed from the perspective of networking. The network effect arises when a large number of individuals share over a connected network. The network amplifies things of interest and provides continuous opportunities for growth and improvement, reinforcing a sense of belonging, removing barriers to information and knowledge, opening up communication and embedding shared beliefs in practices that work.

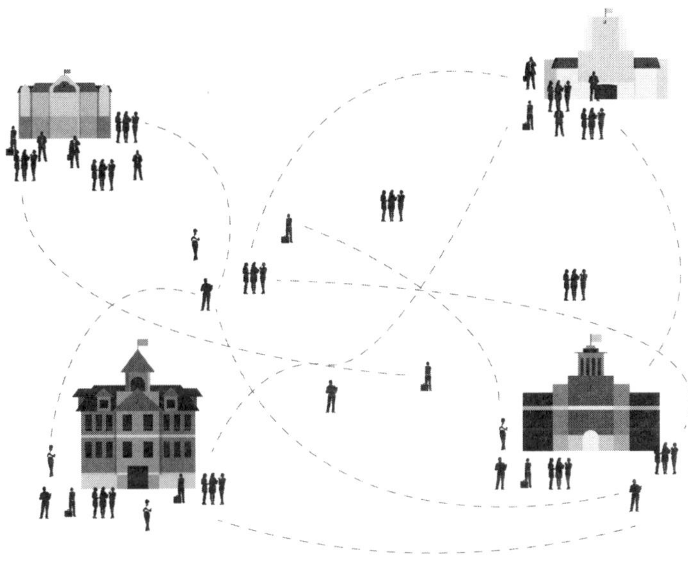

**Figure 8: Networks for professional development of teachers**

An interesting case study of leveraging mentoring models for teacher networks is the Ambience Teacher Mentoring ECHO program[60] anchored by Anuradha Rai, Principal, Ambience Public School, Gurugram, India. The ECHO model, launched in 2003, was originally conceived in the field of medicine helping frontline doctors with sophisticated virtual help from remote specialists. It was adapted to the field of education and brought to India in December 2015 by Rai. Rather than being an

60 Project Echo, Ambience Public School, retrieved on April 30, 2019 from https://www.echoindia.in/partner/ambience-public-school-safdarjung/

inwards focused program for the teachers of the Ambience School, it was designed to be open and inclusive. Teachers from other private and government schools in India have participated in the program, which started with a focus on early literacy and math, and has now expanded to science, well-being and mindfulness, collaborative ECHO, preventive health ECHO, ECHO for building comprehension and writing skills, and storytelling to address the needs of children at risk and to build social cohesion. There are usually two sessions a month in each subject involving preparation, case discussions, modeling of lessons through video and sharing of resources.

Like many other such initiatives, TESS India[61] supports professional teacher development using Open Education Resources (OER). These OERs, aimed at both pre-service and in-service teachers, aim at building effective classroom practice in primary and secondary school teaching using case studies and techniques. Project DIKSHA[62] is a similar initiative for teacher education and professional development launched by the Government of India in 2017. But unless teachers grow their own personal and professional networks of learning and caring, these initiatives may not result in their intended outcomes - simply providing content and mandating certifications alone is not enough.

It is true that the availability of technology, power and connectivity can greatly speed up the network effect. But it is not unwise to consider alternatives when it comes to underserved communities who are as disconnected as can be from the hustle of urban social networks. The alternatives have taken many forms – ranging over village level community radios, mass media, newspapers, phone-based activities, traveling training vans and many self-organized approaches. The continuing enhancement of reach of information technology to the remotest corners of the country offers its own set of future possibilities.

---

61 About Us, TESS-India, retrieved on December 11, 2017 from http://www.tess-india.edu.in/about-tess-india

62 About DISKHA, retrieved on December 11, 2017 from https://diksha.gov.in/#about

The design of these network systems for teacher development can be crucial.[63] The networks must balance between pedagogy and content, teacher and expert, constructed and delivered, and between prescription and adaptation. Another important consideration is that perhaps the networks could individually vary based on their subject focus and their complementarity with other measures to improve schooling outcomes.

Could these networks lead to improved student learning outcomes? Researchers have found that there is an indirect connection. Teachers' networks foster a shared sense of responsibility for positive outcomes and a sense of empowerment through shared practice, improved confidence and better skills. This 'collective efficacy' is both associated with teacher collaboration and student achievement. As Bandura[64] defines it, collective efficacy 'represents a group's shared belief in its conjoint capabilities to organize and execute the courses of action required to produces given levels of attainment'.

An interesting study[65] on teacher networks observes:

> Recent studies have indicated that dense teacher networks around work related advice support an innovative school climate, in which people are willing to take risks to collectively improve educational instruction. Also, teachers who maintained many connections with colleagues and were embedded in a densely connected network displayed higher levels of trust in their colleagues. Both teacher trust and schools' innovative climates have been associated with student achievement.

---

63 McDonald, Joseph P. and Emily J. Klein (2003). Networking for teacher learning: Toward a theory of effective design, New York University, retrieved on September 3, 2017 from http://www.montclair.edu/profilepages/media/1411/user/Networking_for_Teacher_Learning.pdf

64 Bandura, A. (1997). *Self-efficacy: The exercise of control*. New York. NY: W. H. Freeman. pp. 477-478

65 Moolenaar, Nienke M., Peter J.C. Sleegers, Alan J. Daly (2016). Teaming up: Linking collaboration networks, collective efficacy, and student achievement. *Teaching and Teacher Education,* 28 (12) 251-62, Elsevier Ltd, retrieved on August 1, 2018 from https://www.sciencedirect.com/science/article/pii/S0742051X11001156?via%3Dihub

But how should or can these networks or groups be designed? What are the differences to note between networks and groups? How do they evolve over time? How much do they need to be managed and governed?

Downes made very clear distinctions between groups and networks. While groups are characterized by unity, coordination, closed boundaries and centralization, networks are open, diverse, autonomous and connective.[66]

In networks, of particular importance are the density and quality of the interactions within them, the degree of connectedness of participants to others and emergence of local hubs that perform many centralization and aggregation functions. When viewed from the lens of social network analysis and theories around communities and networks of practice, we can see patterns of sub-networks emerge – from diffused sparsely connected networks to denser, more connected sub-networks based on trust and reciprocation.

Members of properly seeded and participative networks exhibit specific kinds of behaviors – self-organization, adaptation and emergence – that give these networks their stability and coherence. These behaviors are explained by Complexity theory, through which the open, dynamic, and networked nature of these networks can be better understood.[67]

What needs emphasizing in such networks is the role of catalytic agents or events – elements that are responsible for connection-making to happen. As described by Moolenaar, Sleegers and Daly, these could be elements of *expressive* social networks - committed and passionate individuals or groups, and content-led or interaction-led mechanisms. These could also be elements of *instrumental* social networks - simply

66 Downes, Stephen (2007, November, 24). Groups vs networks: The class struggle continues, retrieved on December 14, 2017 from http://www.downes.ca/post/42521

67 Morrison, Keith (2006). Complexity theory and education, APERA Conference, retrieved on November 26, 2017 from http://edisdat.ied.edu.hk/pubarch/b15907314/full_paper/SYMPO-000004_Keith%20Morrison.pdf

mandated actions in the network by a position of authority or by rule. In instrumental social networks, the focus is on achieving organizational goals. Expressive social networks rely on the building of trust and social relationships accompanied by empathy. These expressive social networks are found to be more sustainable in practice.

One type of professional development networks is the 'Community of Practice' (CoP), as described by Etienne Wenger.[68] He gives it a formal definition, distinguishing CoPs from interest groups, business/functional units, teams and networks (which he considers as sets of relationships).

What is really interesting is that Wenger has identified five common stages of evolution of a CoP– potential, coalescing, active, dispersed and memorable. The *potential* stage is where members of the community get introduced to each other, share stories and resources, establish a common vision, and set shared goals. The *coalescing* stage is where the community carves out its own identity and establishes value for its members. The *active* stage is where learning and sharing events become structured and periodic, and members actively contribute to its repository of knowledge and practices. The *dispersed* stage is where the community starts dissipating and loses the impetus it had during its formation. The *memorable* stage is when the community is no longer active though it is still remembered as a rich centralized resource. Not all communities of practice will go through all the five stages. Some of them may be kept alive through new leadership and activities. Similarly, there are other models for tracing group or community evolution like George Charrier's Cog's Ladder Model and Bruce Tuckman's five stage model.[69]

---

68 Wenger, Etienne (1998, June). Communities of practice, learning as a social system, retrieved on September 5, 2017 from http://www.providersedge.com/docs/km_articles/CoP_-_Learning_as_a_Social_System.pdf

69 Baxi, Viplav (2008). Groups and Networks: 2.0 Formal Methodologies, *Viplav Baxi's Meanderings*, retrieved on September 5, 2017 from https://learnos.wordpress.com/2008/06/12/groups-and-networks-formal-methodologies/

Wenger[70] also describes some of the roles that exist for internal leadership of the CoP, which he believes are key to its development.

- The inspirational leadership provided by thought leaders and recognized experts
- The day-to-day leadership provided by those who organize activities
- The interpersonal leadership provided by those who weave the community's social fabric
- The boundary leadership provided by those who connect the community to other communities
- The institutional leadership provided by those who maintain links with other organizational constituencies, in particular the official hierarchy

Building upon Wenger's CoPs, Brown and Duguid developed the concept of 'Networks of Practice'[71] to denote people connected together by virtue of a common occupation, practice or knowledge. Such a network emphasizes 'reach over reciprocity', i.e. members are loosely connected to each other via information streams and knowledge stores, unlike in CoPs where relationships are tight-knit and reciprocity is much more important. Networks form and dissipate very regularly, almost in an ad-hoc manner. It is common for activity to surge around an area of common interest, but it lacks the structure and cohesion of groups. Learning is serendipitous, embedded in interactions.

Networks of Practice and Communities of Practice, taken together:

---

70 Baxi, Viplav (2008). Communities of Practice, Learning as a social system (Wenger, 1998), *Viplav Baxi's Meanderings*, retrieved on November 26, 2017 from https://learnos.wordpress.com/2008/07/23/communities-of-practice-learning-as-a-social-system-wenger-1998/

71 Brown, J. S., and Duguid, P. (2000). *The social life of information*, Boston: Harvard Business School Press, p 141

> These two - networks and communities - produce areas marked by a common identity and coordinated practice within any larger network.[72]

It is worthwhile to keep in mind the nature, dynamics and evolution of groups and networks while thinking about the design of such forms of organizations for teachers.

Inasmuch as effective teacher networks could provide the support required in improving teaching, it is possible that learning outcomes may also be impacted positively. With the improvement in communications and the immediacy of instant messaging type of tools, the segments of teachers that have access to the Internet, can benefit immensely. For those that do not have this access, many alternative methods could be deployed.

Irrespective of technology availability, the principles discussed here are important to keep in mind when designing or influencing teacher networks. At scale, this may result in a more durable and democratic solution, far more effective than the traditional top down measures such as mandated training programs. Additionally, if it results in increased capabilities for teachers to explore, contribute and build their own networks, we would have come a long way in teacher continuous professional development.

72 Ibid, p 144

# #5

# What*If*

## every student got a personalized path to mastery of concepts?

# #5 WHAT*IF* EVERY STUDENT GOT A PERSONALIZED PATH TO MASTERY OF CONCEPTS?

*All our classrooms are not just multi-grade but also multi-level. If that is true, how do we ensure that our system of education promotes learning for all? What if students were given new opportunities to learn based on what they want or need? What if teaching and learning could be tailored as per individual preferences? What if instruction could really be differentiated? What if we could flip learning?*

*What if we used intelligence driven computing systems at scale to augment teacher insight? What if these systems enabled students to gain mastery of concepts? What if we could implement these systems at scale?*

Imagine you are teaching a room full of students. You are coping with the pressures of time and curriculum at one end, and the individuality and diversity of your students at the other. Not all of your students are brilliant performers, at least not yet. So you have to cope with students who need more guidance and support, alongside those who are self-driven and proficient at learning. There is a large 'middle' – moderately performing students. Your class size is fairly large. It is not the only class you teach; there are more like this one. In fact, you teach more than just one group of students each day. As a result, you have limited time and opportunities to spend time with each sub-group in your classroom, and far less time to focus on individual differences in ability or interest. What would your strategy for teaching be? What help would you need?

We know that each child is different in terms of her learning needs, attitudes and growth. However, many education systems literally force teachers to 'teach to the middle', wherever that 'middle' is, because they give little flexibility, time, tools, and autonomy to them to experiment with and implement personalized approaches.

The realization that every child is different is daunting for a teacher. It is easy to understand and appreciate, but challenging to address as an issue. It is complicated by the group dynamics in a classroom and constrained by the demands of the age-leveled curricula and system of exams. For most practical purposes, it is sometimes considered a problem too complex to solve within the parameters of the current systems of education, thereby also dismissing the possible solutions with it. We live by our approximations and cannot get too deterministic about what we expect to happen.

A lot of research has already been done into making teaching-learning both personalized and personal. Some examples include pedagogies for mixed ability classrooms such as differentiated instruction and multi-grade multi-level techniques, the emergence of second-generation (connectionist) Artificial Intelligence based intelligent teaching-learning systems backed by Big Data and machine learning, and the research and practice on models of social and networked learning, backed by the theory of Connectivism.

## THE MGML APPROACH

Multi-grade, multi-level (MGML) classrooms group students by ability rather than age, using a variety of techniques for curriculum organization and teaching such as common timetables, subject-stagger, and subject-grouping options. A Zambian report[73] finds that there are some challenges such as lack of formal recognition, stigma of teaching in remote areas, insufficient resources and overstretched teachers. But despite these constraints, multi-grade teaching is an effective way to address, at least, the needs of students within a class.

> It can enhance independent learning, it encourages teachers to adopt pupil-centered approaches to teaching, it facilitates revision of materials covered in earlier grades, it increases pupil interaction, and contributes to the country's objective of universalizing basic education.

This is a more widespread and under-served phenomenon than we perhaps realize, the world over. MGML classrooms have been a reality for thousands of years – we just need to look at the ancient *Gurukul* system in India to see how courses were tailored to individual abilities – they could be completed as per the individual capacity of the students. In fact, it is said that Lord Krishna completed his course of studies in sixty-four days![74]

In a report on the MGML efforts in India, Radhika Herzberger traces the origins of MGML to the Rishi Valley school of India.[75] Mono-grade approaches were found to be inadequate for multi-grade classrooms.

---

73 History of multi-grade teaching in Zambia, Peter Merckx and Teacher Education Department, Lusaka, retrieved on August 15, 2017 from http://multigrade01.tripod.com/id2.html

74 Rangan, R (2012). Literary research on gurukula education system and yoga: a comparison of cognitive functions of yoga based gurukul education system and modern education system, Chapter 2, retrieved on April 30, 2019 from https://sg.inflibnet.ac.in/jspui/bitstream/10603/7707/8/08_chapter%202.pdf

75 Herzberger, Radhika (undated) Brief history of multigrade-multilevel methodology practiced at Rishi Valley and its environs, retrieved on August 4, 2018 from https://whatifedu.files.wordpress.com/2018/08/history-of-mgml-at-rishi-valley.pdf

> …surveys of schools in the Indian countryside point to large-scale failure rates due largely to the practice of a pedagogy based on monograde principles practiced in schools the majority of which are multigrade.

This idea evolved into RIVER, (Rishi Valley Institute of Educational Resources), an initiative to handle precisely this issue. Over the years, RIVER has reached 13 Indian states covering around 34,000 schools, 1.3 million students and about 68,000 teachers in 2015-16 and nearly 20.5 million children and 911,000 teachers cumulatively since 2006-07.[76] It has spread across Indian boundaries to countries as diverse as Ethiopia, Germany, Bangladesh, and Nepal. The outcomes are quite impressive. It has been found that average achievement of children increased by 25-29 percent, above 80 percent of parents felt no pressure in exam preparation, students displayed increased confidence and there was immense buy-in from teachers.

But how did this work in practice? The approach to teaching and learning followed in the RIVER model is quite interesting. Faced with students with differing abilities and interests, they decided to break down the curriculum into smaller learning units that were more manageable for students. These learning units allowed the student to demonstrate a specific competency or learning outcome, also called a 'milestone'. For each subject, these milestones were arranged logically in a sequence from lower to higher levels of complexity and difficulty. This sequence was called a 'learning ladder'.

Within a milestone, materials and activities were arranged so that students went through an introduction to the concept, then applied it through practice, underwent evaluations and associated remediation if required, and subsequently were guided to enrichment activities and further exploration. These activities were organized in the form of learning 'cards' that were made available in a structured manner to students so that they could easily access them when they needed.

---

76 Report on MGML reach and impact, RIVER, retrieved on April 30, 2019 from https://whatifedu.files.wordpress.com/2018/08/03_report-on-river-mgml-reach-and-impact.pdf

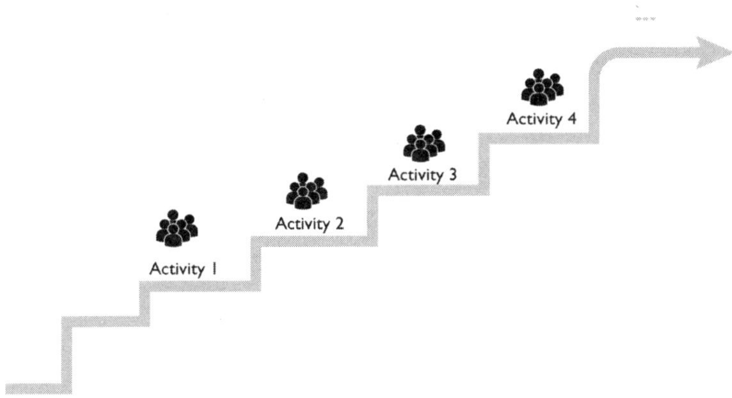


**Figure 9: Activity based learning methods**

Each child started at the bottom of the learning ladder with an initial set of activities. She would take the learning card and find a place in the room to complete it. When she completed one set of activities, she could pick the second one, and so on. This way she could navigate the syllabus a ladder rung at a time. Teachers would demystify activities, guide and mentor the child, and assess progress at each point. They would provide the necessary remediation if the child had problems completing the task.

Teachers took ownership of the curriculum and how it was to be implemented. They created their own materials and adapted them as they went along. There was little or no reliance on textbooks. Classrooms provided the choice of flexible seating. Evaluation was a continuous process. Children took charge of their own learning, at their own pace. This reduced, to a very large extent, the anxiety of performance and fear in the classroom.[77]

This card-ladder approach was used as a basis for the Activity Based Learning (ABL) method by the flagship primary schools program of the Indian government, Sarva Shiksha Abhiyan (literally 'education for all'),

77 Characteristics of the MGML methodology, RIVER, retrieved on September 15, 2017 from http://river-rv.blogspot.in/2009/03/characteristics-of-mgml-methodology.html

and soon to 13 states. In 2013, a UNICEF report[78] investigated the effectiveness of the ABL method as it was implemented at 857 schools across seven Indian states.

Was it possible that this model had really scaled effectively? The report found that learning outcomes had significantly increased, but only where implementation met certain criteria. The ABL method, when implemented properly, showed significant improvements in both general classroom indicators and learning outcomes. Classrooms that used the card-ladder model for grouping students were half a standard deviation ahead of classrooms that did not, and classrooms where there was a high usage of the learning materials were a third of a standard deviation ahead in performance.

But implementation has not scaled well at all. Actual adoption has been very low. For example, despite four States mandating the card-ladder model, only 23 percent of the classrooms actually practiced it. The proper training of teachers and ensuring their buy-in, commitment, and discipline in using the method could not be ensured. There was much more focus on procedure rather than on the underlying principles. Schools that adopted textbooks muted the autonomy and control that children needed to have in negotiating their own learning. The design of activities did not promote active reflection, an essential part of the card-ladder method.

Teachers who did believe that the card-ladder approach could work, a small fraction of all teachers conducting this method in these schools, were able to demonstrate significantly higher learning outcomes. But the large majority of teachers and schools did not appreciate and actively understand the model. Consequently ABL learning materials had low overall usage in the classroom. To compound these issues, the problems of high pupil-teacher ratios, unavailability of infrastructure or

78 UNICEF (2013). Child friendly learning in India: A model for child friendly education, policy brief, UNICEF

adequate numbers of teachers and the frequent changes in the design also impacted the implementation.

## COMMUNITY APPROACHES

A similar approach is followed by Pratham Education Foundation, the progenitors of the Annual Status of Education Reports (ASER) for India. Their initiative, 'Teaching at the Right Level' (TaRL),[79] attempts to teach children at the learning level they are at, rather than by age or grade linked levels. They identify the students' current learning levels, group them accordingly, assign teachers to these groups and equip them with the appropriate teaching material, and monitor student progress. TaRL has been implemented in a variety of modes, in-school and out of school, and with both teachers and community volunteers. Since 2010, about 13.8 million children have participated in TaRL programs in India, making it one of the largest implementations of such a method, perhaps anywhere in the world.[80]

> The Learning camp model, implemented directly by Pratham staff with assistance from locally recruited and trained volunteers, provides intensive bursts of instruction in math and hindi for eight to 10 days at a time for up to two months. Students in grades 3-5 are grouped according to learning levels (i.e. whether they can read letters, words, sentences, paragraphs, etc.) and are taught using level-appropriate materials tailored for each group.

The Learning Camp model is an interesting one from the perspective of parental and community participation in education. If worked on in concert with classroom teaching and with the help of local community volunteers, it can greatly support individualized learning.

79 Teaching at the right level: summary of interventions, Pratham, retrieved on November 26, 2017 from http://pratham.org/templates/pratham/images/Evaluations_of_Pratham_Teaching_at_the_Right_Level_TaRL_programs_by_J-PAL.pdf

80 Remedial Education, Abdul Latif Jameel Poverty Action Lab, retrieved on July 14, 2018 from https://www.povertyactionlab.org/scale-ups/remedial-education

Another example of that approach is 826 National,[81] a movement started by Dave Eggers and Ninive Calegari in the USA, to provide after-school support for creative writing. They addressed students in the 6-18 years age group. Their model was simple. They recognized that students needed individual attention in exciting and authentic non-classroom situations. They set up free local centers where professionals and volunteers could spend whatever dedicated time they could find, to work with individual students and help them overcome their challenges in writing.

Over time, since 2002, the number of centers has grown to 826 chapters in seven cities across the country. They serve over 30,000 students and offer 'after-school tutoring, field trips, workshops, Young Authors' Book Project, and in-school programs — all free of charge — for students, classes, and schools'. By providing a third place (away from school and home) of learning, project based techniques, and a culture of creativity, 826 National chapters have demonstrated the power of the community to impact student performance. Their efforts have directly resulted in a marked improvement in the ability and readiness of students for the traditional school programs.

The team at 826 National recognized that it is important to consider current classrooms in schools as Single Grade Multi-Level classrooms (SGML) or 'mixed ability classrooms'. This means that even while students get slotted in classes according to their age, we need to address the variance in ability across and within their classrooms more effectively. While they provided a third site of learning away from the school, they also partnered with local schools and adjusted their programs to resolve specific pain points that the schools shared with them. In this way, both the schools and the students benefited.

These are important considerations. About 10 percent of India's primary schools are single teacher schools running multi-grade class-

81 About 826 and 826 National, retrieved on December 2, 2017 from https://826national.org/about/

rooms. About 33 percent of Indian schools have an enrolment of less than 50 students. A whopping 85 percent of schools are located in rural areas.[82] The discussion around MGML and SGML classrooms assumes great importance for India, as it does for many developing countries facing similar constraints and challenges.

A UNESCO report found that in India in 1996, 84 percent of the primary schools had three teachers or less (in 2015-16, the nationwide average was 3.1). They found that national micpolicies imposed mono-grade practices on multi-grade classroom schools. When they studied MGML schools, they found that these schools expanded access to schooling (an important contribution towards meeting the goal of universal education), positively impacted the cognitive achievements of learners and had positive social and personal effects on learners. They afforded opportunities for learners to develop self-study skills, helped them establish a collective responsibility for learning across age levels and enabled remediation through peer tutoring. Their recommendation was that national policies must directly support MGML practices in an integrated manner, including making relevant changes in curriculum, learning materials, teacher education and assessment methods.[83]

## OTHER MODELS OF INSTRUCTION

There is substantial work that has been done which can guide how teachers can meet these challenges. According to Carol Tomlinson,[84] who proposed the technique of Differentiated Instruction:

---

82 UDISE (2016). Elementary education in India: Progress towards UEE, U-DISE Flash Statistics 2015-16, National University of Education and Planning, New Delhi, India

83 Little, Angela W (2004). Learning and teaching in multigrade settings, Paper prepared for the UNESCO 2005 EFA Monitoring Report, retrieved on August 15, 2017 from http://siteresources.worldbank.org/INTINDIA/4371432-1194542398355/21543231/LearningandTeachinginMulti-Gradeclassrooms.pdf

84 Tomlinson, Carol and Susan Allan (2000). Leadership for *differentiating* schools and classrooms, *ASCD, retrieved on April 30, 2019 from* http://www.ascd.org/publications/books/100216.aspx

> The idea of differentiating instruction to accommodate the different ways that students learn involves a hefty dose of common sense, as well as sturdy support in the theory and research of education. It is an approach to teaching that advocates active planning for student differences in classrooms.

The Differentiated Instruction model depends on several key elements such as a high quality curriculum, continual assessment, respectful tasks, building communities, flexible grouping and teaching up (going beyond the comfort level of the students through challenging tasks and encouraging hard work). Essentially, it moves away from a one-size-fits-all approach or even a pre-fixed conception of ability levels of students (say, based on level of difficulty), to much more emphasis on being aware of each child's progress, learning preferences and behavior.[85] It gives students more control of and awareness about their goals, the groups they participate in and the progress they make. This model provides guidance to teachers on how to manage the diversity in the classroom.[86] Content is differentiated based on the current level of knowledge and ability. For example, a class would have some students with little or no appreciation of the subject, others that would be proficient at the subject, and the remaining who would fall between these two categories.

The teacher could then tailor the activities provided for each segment – starting from lower level activities involving remembering and understanding, to more complex activities that entail evaluating and synthesizing ideas. She could also differentiate on the basis of learning styles and orientations. Students may work better with others or by themselves, or by using a particular mode of learning that meets their

85 What is differentiated instruction?, Differentiation Central, Institutes on Academic Diversity in the Curry School of Education at the University of Virginia, retrieved on September 10, 2017 from http://differentiationcentral.com/what-is-differentiated-instruction/

86 Weselby, Cathy (2014). What is differentiated instruction? Examples of How to Differentiate Instruction in the Classroom, retrieved on December 2, 2017 from https://education.cu-portland.edu/blog/classroom-resources/examples-of-differentiated-instruction/

preferred styles. The teacher may even customize the final product of their learning according to what works for them, for example through a quiz, a project or an essay. She may configure her classroom physically to allow breakouts, quiet corners, and one on one interactions.

Another possible model is team teaching, also known as collaborative or co-teaching proposed in 1963 by William Alexander, father of the 'American Middle School.'[87] In this model, two or more teachers work collaboratively to teach a larger group of students. The teachers need to work with each other, leverage their unique strengths and perspectives, and plan their interactions with individual students and groups. They may bring in cross-disciplinary linkages by integrating their subject areas into common themes. They may choose to schedule their classes differently as well – combining sessions or sequencing them adjacently.

Another approach is the flipped classroom method evolved by Aaron Sams.[88] He 'flipped' or inverted the traditional teaching model. Instead of lecturing in the classroom, Aaron asked his students to view his lecture videos at home. When they came to class, they would collaboratively solve problems, resolve doubts and learn new content. There are many other 'flips' such as the following that we could imagine.[89]

- Students into teachers
- Homework into classwork
- Classwork into learning by self or network, guided or unguided
- Hallways and social spaces into classrooms

---

87 Gayton, Jorge (2010). Instructional Strategies to accommodate a team teaching approach, Business Communication Quarterly, SAGE Publications, retrieved on 22 July, 2018 from http://journals.sagepub.com/doi/abs/10.1177/1080569909358097

88 Putting students at the center, TechSmith, retrieved on December 2, 2017 from https://www.techsmith.com/flipped-classroom-aaron-sams.html

89 Baxi, Viplav (2012). Unflipping the Flip, *Viplav Baxi's Meanderings*, retrieved on December 2, 2017 from https://learnos.wordpress.com/2012/07/09/unflipping-the-flip/

- Closed curriculum to open
- Degrees to badges
- Fixed learning periods to flexible learning time, anywhere
- Fellow students into collaborators

Flipped learning and teaching models have been found effective in increasing student engagement, motivation, and performance.[90]

Can the teaching-learning alternatives discussed thus far be tailored to suit individual needs? Can these approaches scale over large numbers of teachers and students in a way that is consistent with the (at least) avowed goals of our education systems?

## THE PERSONAL AND PERSONALIZED

There is a wide spectrum of approaches to tailor learning and instruction, from mass-stereotyping of learners (for example, by age), to segmenting learners by ability into groups, and finally to completely personalized learning for each individual – a range from the collective to the individual.

The mass stereotyping occurs when the same levels of knowledge acquisition and performative (read, outcome based) learning levels are designed and mandated for all learners belonging to a defined class irrespective of individual differences. In this case, whether the curriculum is influenced by one particular theory of learning or another, it basically caters to a global minimum expectation from the system. These expectations are called learning outcomes. On the other extreme of the spectrum, the completely personalized learning models focus on tailoring the process to every individual's specific needs. They adapt curricula to the behavior and progress of the students.

90 10 Published Results Supporting the Benefits of Flipped Learning, FLIP Learning, retrieved on December 2, 2017 from http://www.flippedclassroomworkshop.com/results-studies-supporting-benefits-of-flipped-classroom/

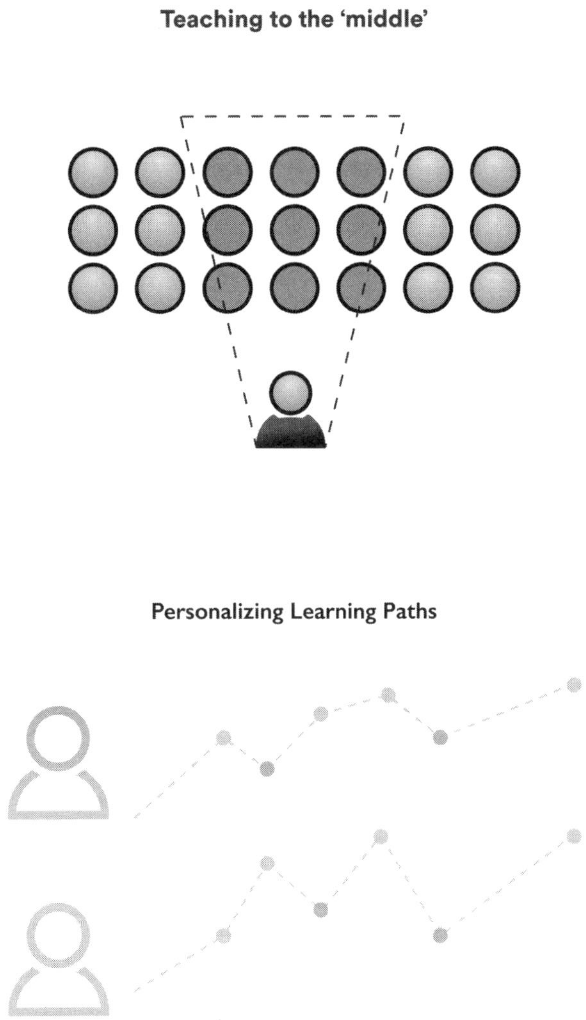


**Figure 10: Homogenized vs. Differentiated teaching and learning**

The impact of learning theories is manifested in the design of curricula, the training of teachers, and the design of assessments. Some theories focus on behavior, some on cognitive models of learning, some around the socially and historically contextualized and experiential models of learning, and some around the networked and connected models of learning. In general, these theories of learning often provide some specific cues to teach and learn, and are of great importance when designing personalized systems of learning.

Various people have tried to address this problem of personalization. At the mass stereotype level, undoubtedly the biggest contributor would have to be psychologist B.F. Skinner who, through his various experiments with behavior, evolved a theory of learning called Behaviorism. Building on the conditioned reflex theory of Ivan Pavlov,[91] who observed that there is a natural reflex exhibited when a certain stimulus is presented, Skinner showed that it was possible for behavior to be programmed if there was an added feedback mechanism. That is, given certain stimuli with an accompanying reward or punishment and with appropriate reinforcement, we could provoke learning. Example demonstrations included pigeons playing ping-pong (Project Pigeon) and rats pulling levers (the Skinner Box).[92]

Using this approach, Skinner created the 'teaching box', a technique that emulated the working of a behaviorist teacher.

> Skinner believed using his teaching machine to break down material bit by bit, offering rewards along the way for correct responses, could serve almost like a private tutor for students. Material was presented in sequence, and the machine provided hints and suggestions until students verbally explained a response to a problem (Skinner didn't believe in multiple choice answers). The device wouldn't allow students to move on in a lesson until they understood the material, and when students got any part of it right, the machine would spit out positive feedback until they reached the solution. The teaching box didn't stick in a school setting, but many computer-based self-instruction programs today use the same idea.

91 Ivan Pavlov, retrieved on September 16, 2017 from https://en.wikipedia.org/wiki/Ivan_Pavlov

92 B.F. Skinner: The man who taught pigeons to play ping-pong and rats to pull levers, *Smithsonian Mag*, retrieved on September 16, 2017 from http://www.smithsonianmag.com/science-nature/bf-skinner-the-man-who-taught-pigeons-to-play-ping-pong-and-rats-to-pull-levers-5363946

The allusion to multiple choice answers is interesting because in 1924, Sidney L Pressey invented a teaching machine that relied on these types of answers.

> Teaching machines are unique among instructional aids in that the student not merely passively listens, watches, or reads but actively responds. And as he does so, he finds out whether his response is correct or not. And a record may be kept which aids in improving the materials.[93]

Pressey's teaching machine, the Automatic Teacher, was designed to help students perform drill and practice at their own pace.

> 'Within the next twenty years,' he predicted, 'special mechanical aids will make mass psychological experimentation commonplace and bring about in education something analogous to the Industrial Revolution.
>
> ...There must be an "industrial revolution" in education in which educational science and the ingenuity of educational technology combine to modernize the grossly inefficient and clumsy procedures of conventional education.'[94]

Pressey designed the Automatic Teacher device to allow personalized instruction for the student, while the teacher was free to concentrate on individual areas with students. But it was a technology that was vigorously resisted and failed to generate enough momentum.

A corollary approach is Programmed Instruction.[95] There are three models of programmed instruction – linear (Skinner), branching (Crowder) and Mathetics (Gilbert). Skinner treated the learning process as a linear one. The linear model consisted of providing instruction in small units,

---

93 Clark, Don (1995). Pressey's teaching machine, retrieved on September 16, 2017 from http://www.nwlink.com/~donclark/hrd/history/machine.html

94 Stephen, Petrina (2004). Sidney Pressey and the automation of education, 1924–1934, *Project MUSE,* retrieved on September 16, 2017 from https://www.academia.edu/5065516/Sidney_Pressey_and_the_Automation_of_Education_1924_1934

95 Programmed Learning, Britannica, retrieved on September 16, 2017 from https://www.britannica.com/topic/programmed-learning

immediate feedback and reinforcement, based on content created by the programmer. Treating the learning process as 'branched' instead of a linear sequence, Crowder advocated a problem solving approach following an exposition-diagnosis-remediation structure, within which the student response dictated which remedial content was to be presented. The third approach, Mathetics, relies on systematically moving from the complex ending concept to its simpler parts.

The introduction of branching made non-linear jumps and cross-referencing possible for the self-paced learner. The student would start by answering a question. If the answer was correct, she would move on to the next question. If she made a mistake, she would be taken to a branch that made her realize her mistake. This process would continue till her misconceptions were resolved or a designed end 'node' was reached in the instruction. Once the misconceptions were resolved, she could move back to the question and re-attempt it. In this way, she could move non-linearly through the answer options, and be allowed to learn from her mistakes, something that a purely linear system would not be able to achieve.

The clear benefits of branching are that they encourage critical thinking, rather than rote learning. The Skinner methods are perhaps more applicable in situations where rote is required, while the Crowder methods are perhaps more applicable to situations where higher order thinking skills are required.

To understand more closely what is meant by 'higher-order' thinking skills, it is important to review Benjamin Bloom's taxonomy of educational objectives, released in 1956,[96] that has played a dominant role in the design of both assessments and content. Bloom and his colleagues worked on defining a shared vocabulary between curriculum

---

96 Armstrong, Patricia. Bloom's Taxonomy. Center for Teaching, Vanderbilt University, retrieved on October 2, 2017 from https://cft.vanderbilt.edu/guides-sub-pages/blooms-taxonomy/

designers and exam designers. The idea was simple. If the curriculum could be broken down into learning objectives and tests could be conducted against those learning objectives in a way that did not involve subjective interpretation, we could have a much desired consistency between the two. But that would require an agreement into the 'verbs' that constitute the language used in stating the learning objective.

For example, at the end of a learning unit, a learning objective could be framed as such: the student should be able to 'compare between (x) and (y)' where x and y are two comparable things that are the subject of the learning unit. The use of the verb 'compare' illustrates 'comprehension' of the topic, one of the six levels that Bloom defined. If both curriculum designers and test creators agreed on this verb as part of their shared vocabulary, they would create content (such a comparison table) to be memorized and understood, and design questions (such as 'compare between x and y') to test if the student really has comprehended the topic. In this manner, Bloom defined six levels of learning/ assessment verbs that have become the default way to frame both learning objectives and assessments.

The first three levels have been popularly called Lower Order Thinking skills or LOTs, and the next three levels have been called Higher Order Thinking skills or HOTs. The LOTs include knowledge, comprehension and application skills (or remembering, comprehending and applying in the revised Bloom's taxonomy that appeared in 2001). The HOTs include analysis, synthesis and evaluation (or analyzing, evaluating and creating in the revised taxonomy). The LOTs are generally considered in a linear manner while the HOTs are considered to operate in parallel, but the interplay between all six levels is easily identifiable if we look at the overall process of learning.

This taxonomy has given a clear point of reference for educators, students, and parents and is followed worldwide. The taxonomy has been useful in standardizing content and assessments. It has also been adopted by the proponents of personalized learning because the learning objectives, their sequencing in a curriculum, and the ability to put a test to each one of them, makes it possible to build adaptive learning experiences.

Where Skinner imagined a set of discrete, linear steps towards completing a learning objective, Crowder imagined a discrete set of branches managed by the logic of programmed instruction. Skinner's teaching model predicated that each student would follow the same path to mastery, while Crowder's model anticipated mistakes. Skinner's model told the student that it was the wrong way to respond, but it was Crowder's model that told them why and proceeded to remedy their mistakes.

Programmed instruction and the work on teaching machines were further augmented by the development of Intelligent Tutoring Systems (ITS)[97] through the rest of the 20th century, and by the evolution of the field of Artificial Intelligence. The ITS modeled both the knowledge domain and the student profile. In the knowledge domain, they included a complete map of the task or concept being taught and captured possible errors or deviations from the ideal path to solve a problem. So, for example, if the task was to add a sequence of numbers correctly, the ITS would also handle situations that could elicit student misconceptions, in problem areas such as carryovers, addition of mixed positive and negative numbers, large and small number problems or small/large number of terms. At each step, misconceptions or possible errors such as calculation mistakes, term grouping, and the ability to handle multiple positive/negative signs in front of a term, would be captured and remedied.

The ITS also modeled the tutor (pedagogical flow) and the student interface (communications for feedback and presentation of hints, for example). The ITS presents the concept and then tasks the student with solving a problem based on the concept. Based on the student's response, the ITS helps identify what the misconception is and proceeds

97 Artificial intelligence, foundations of computational agents, retrieved on October 2, 2017 from http://artint.info/html/ArtInt_27.html

to resolve that, again through a sequence, branch or hierarchy of steps. Once a concept is mastered, students move on to the next one in the sequence. The inter-connections and dependencies between concepts is an integral part of the design (knowledge graph) of the ITS. Some instances of ITS were also known as Cognitive Tutors,[98] since they depended upon modeling the knowledge schema and reinforcing that schema or mental model in the mind of the student through immediate feedback and remediation.

An early example is Ms Lindquist,[99] an algebra tutor program that could carry on a controlled conversation, probe a student's understanding of a concept, identify issues, remedy those issues and provide feedback, much like the real teacher which it was based on.[100] Research in the effectiveness showed that it increased engagement, and improved the experience because it asked questions rather than telling students what the answers were.

Older ITS systems were notoriously difficult, time consuming, and costly to create and required serious skills in programming, subject matter and teaching. However the beginning of the 21st century has seen the resurgence of Artificial Intelligence, specifically around machine learning and the increased availability of low cost highly scalable computing power. It has enabled a newer, easier and more cost effective way of designing programmed instruction. The essential idea is that machines can learn from the behavior of students (or agents) interacting with content. The advances in computing power and the vastly lower costs, has made it possible for a machine to learn over millions of interaction inputs and to also be able to predict errors that could be made by a student. This

---

98 Cognitive Tutor, retrieved on October 7, 2017 from Wikipedia, https://en.wikipedia.org/wiki/Cognitive_tutor

99 Ms. Lindquist: The tutor, retrieved on November 26, 2017 from http://www.cs.cmu.edu/~neil/

100 A comparison of an expert human tutor with a real student and Ms. Lindquist's ability to match that closely, retrieved on November 26, 2017 from http://www.cs.cmu.edu/~neil/comparison.html

is in contrast to the first generation of ITS where the tasks and errors needed to be mapped out in advance. In this new generation of ITS, machines could reliably diagnose, predict and remediate learning errors without explicitly identifying them.

A simple instance of using machine-learning was to identify a cat from prior exposure to millions of images containing a cat. Once the machine was 'trained' on these inputs, it could reliably predict the outputs – which meant that if the machine could be trained on different student interactions with the content, it could safely and reliably be expected to provide the right kind of remediation.

The basic design of the modern ITS consists of three things. A system to handle content typically architected as a graph of concepts linked to each other (the links being relationships such as dependencies and prerequisites), a system to profile the learner -- her context and learning activity, and a system to determine the flow of interaction from a pedagogical perspective. There are many approaches such as similarity-based learning (an approach in supervised machine learning that attempts to check the [dis]similarity between two 'things'), explanation-based learning (an approach in machine learning that allows learning by example, for instance in natural language processing) and case-based learning (the use of existing cases to solve new problems).

The creation of such systems has become easier through services like DialogFlow (earlier Api.ai)[101] and Amazon Lex,[102] that are tools powered by Natural Language Understanding (NLU) and Automated Speech Recognition (ASR), and help to author decision tree based conversation flows for digital virtual robots (bots). These tools allow inputs in natural language determine the intent behind that input and fulfill the intent using custom built logic. These tools also allow chaining of inputs

101 DialogFlow, retrieved on November 16, 2017 from https://dialogflow.com/

102 What is Amazon Lex, retrieved on November 16, 2017 from http://docs.aws.amazon.com/lex/latest/dg/what-is.html

as well, which gives them the ability to build context and to leverage that context in determining how to respond.

Gordon Pask[103], one of the founding fathers of Cybernetics, is credited with making the first adaptive teaching machine in 1956, called SAKI (self-adaptive keyboard instructor). This was the first instance where a machine adapted to the pace and flow of a student's interaction and adjusted the training accordingly[104]. The new machine-learning based systems have resulted in a second wave of ITS based systems, also called Adaptive Learning systems. At the simplest level, these systems deal with a statistical analysis of data and make predictions (or matches). At the more complex levels, these systems (also known as deep learning systems) treat knowledge as a multi-layered network, with backwards (feedback) and forwards (signals) propagation between inputs and outputs. Rather than simple or complex, linear or non-linear relationships between inputs and outputs, the deep learning systems infuse entire networks of variables and relationships in between the inputs and outputs, similar to the human brain (which is why they are also called *neural* networks).

Baker argues that we should also be looking at 'Stupid' Tutoring Systems[105] – systems that report out issues to 'intelligent' humans, who can then make decisions on what to do to solve the problems of the student. Some of this work has already been done, for example, in the Purdue Course Signals initiative[106] which provided teachers with insight on at-risk students. He cogently argues that the goal of AI or machine

---

103 Scott, Bernard (1996, April 12). Obituary: Professor Gordon Pask, Independent, retrieved on April 30, 2019 from https://www.independent.co.uk/news/people/obituary-professor-gordon-pask-1304435.html

104 Watters, Audrey (2018). Teaching Machines: An American Story (And the Case for Gordon Pask), retrieved on August 08, 2018 from http://teachingmachin.es/2018/08/08/update

105 Baker, Ryan S. (2016). Stupid tutoring systems, intelligent humans, retrieved on November 26, 2017 from http://radix.www.upenn.edu/learninganalytics/ryanbaker/STS-Baker-IJAIED-v15.pdf

106 CASE STUDY A: Traffic lights and interventions: Signals at Purdue University, Learning Analytics in Higher Education, A review of UK and international practice, JISC, retrieved on November 26, 2017 from https://analytics.jiscinvolve.org/wp/files/2016/04/CASE-STUDY-A-Purdue-University.pdf

learning is not to design intelligent systems, but to create systems that build and leverage human intelligence – 'stupid tutoring systems and intelligent humans'.

## IMPACT OF NETWORKS

In parallel, building on the nascent science of networks (Network Science), researchers have started applying social network analysis (SNA) techniques to educational settings. Essentially SNA is used to explain and predict network behavior.

> Social network analysis [SNA] is the mapping and measuring of relationships and flows between people, groups, organizations, computers, URLs, and other connected information/knowledge entities.[107]

SNA can be used to describe many real world phenomena such as the spread of a disease, terror networks[108] and voting.[109] Of particular importance is the concept of *wirearchy* proposed by Valdis Krebs[110] in the context of organizational networks. As opposed to hierarchical organizations, wirearchy is the idea of an emergent organization, the structures that emerge during the course of everyday interaction between people. This idea is also relevant to our discussions on groups and networks in education because it demonstrates that in addition to top down designs of groups in the traditional systems, there are other structures that emerge out of interactions between students, parents, and teachers that are not designed or available at the outset. This has

---

107 Social network analysis: an introduction, retrieved on November 26, 2017 from http://www.orgnet.com/sna.html

108 Krebs, Valdis (2006). Connecting the dots, tracking two identified terrorists, retrieved on November 26, 2017 from http://www.orgnet.com/tnet.html

109 Krebs, Valdis (2015). It's the conversations, stupid! The link between social interaction and political choice, retrieved on November 26, 2017 from http://www.extremedemocracy.com/chapters/Chapter%20Nine-Krebs.pdf

110 Krebs, Valdis and Jon Husband (2015). Networks and wirearchy, Workforce Solutions, *Review*, retrieved on November 26, 2017 from http://orgnet.com/WSR_July2015Krebs-Husband.pdf

direct implications on how teachers, for example, could organize groups in MGML classrooms, and how students could self-organize into smaller collaborative groups.

The adaptation of some of these techniques in education has given rise to the field of Learning Analytics (LA).[111] The practitioners of LA believe it is distinctly different from the more traditional field of academic analytics that a majority of institutions follow. To differentiate between the two:[112]

> Learning analytics (LA) is the measurement, collection, analysis and reporting of data about learners and their contexts, for purposes of understanding and optimizing learning and the environments in which it occurs. Academic analytics is the improvement of organizational processes, workflows, resource allocation, and institutional measurement through the use of learner, academic, and institutional data.

Learning analytics relate to making learners successful, while academic analytics relate to improving organizational effectiveness. LA enables you to capture data on learning and teaching from a variety of sources and at many levels – for example, personal, social, course and departmental. It is focused on learners and educators and is used to generate actionable insights into classroom and course level activities. From a technology architecture perspective, LA is very similar to the design of ITS, insofar as it adopts modern technologies, cloud computing, social networks and machine learning as its tools.

If the way we capture student interactions with content and assessments is changed, we must bring about changes in the way content and assessment are accessed, conducted, and tracked. It is equally necessary, if learning is to be made adaptive that teaching, assessment and content also adapt to the insights generated by LA. For example, teachers would

---

111 Society for Learning Analytics research, SoLAR, retrieved on October 7, 2017 from https://solaresearch.org/

112 Open learning analytics: An integrated & modularized platform, SoLAR, retrieved on April 30, 2019 from http://solaresearch.org/wp-content/uploads/2011/12/OpenLearningAnalytics.pdf

no longer teach with monolithic lesson plans, would less regularly plan whole-class activities, would use data to determine teaching approaches and techniques, and will use tools to let students achieve guided mastery in a blended manner. Similarly, publishers will need to create content in such a manner that it can be available for remediation, just in time.

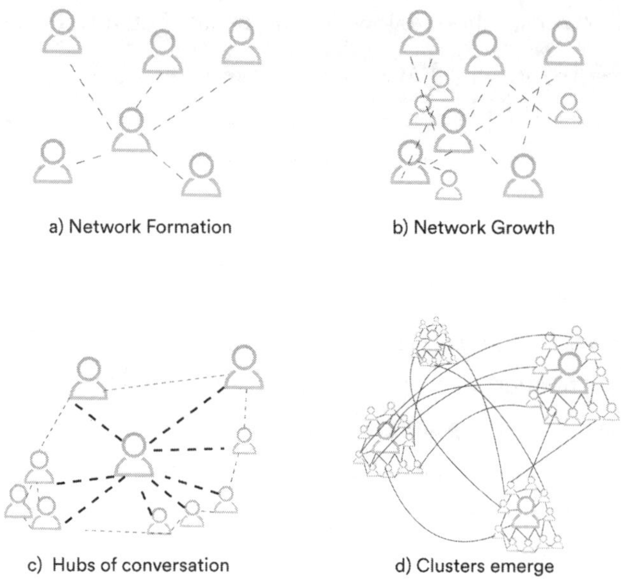


**Figure 11: The evolution of networks of learning and teaching**

The advances in computing technology now enable us to quickly and affordably add intelligence to the teaching learning process. This can only be realized in practice, if we supply millions of data points to these engines to become better and more reliable.

The siloed, isolated nature of classroom instruction makes this near impossible to scale. But if teachers start adopting these techniques to augment their classroom teaching, we will take a giant step towards solving the mixed-ability issue at scale. It would also be important to consider modeling class interactions in a deeper and more meaningful manner for the teacher and her students, in a way that it becomes simpler for a teacher to accommodate diversity in teaching and learning experiences and to adapt to individual needs.

Of course, this also means considerable investment in building access to digital resources and in research and development. Equally important is how we will secure data and ensure privacy. But if we want to efficiently and accurately tackle the challenge of scale and provide an individualized path to mastery for each student, this should become an extremely important focus area for us. Perhaps it is imperative now to consider such practices in mixed-ability classrooms by leveraging education technology, advances in pedagogy and assessments, learning analytics and better infrastructure available today.

# #6

# What*If*

## we changed the way we credential learners?

# #6 WHAT *IF* WE CHANGED THE WAY WE CREDENTIAL LEARNERS?

*Is our system of credentialing truly reflective of the abilities and interests of our students? What if we move away from our pre-occupation with degrees and diplomas and consider alternative credentialing systems? What if we consciously eliminate the stress and fear of traditional examinations?*

*What if we use badging and gamification techniques to increase a sense of achievement and mastery? What if we adapt content and instruction to foster emergent capabilities rather than prescribed ones? What if we design credentialing to respect individual ability and acknowledge differences? What if we could inspire learning through an effective system of rewards?*

Place yourself in the role of an agency defining the system of education. You have already established the institutional structures, the disciplines you will focus on, the curricula, the way you organize students into groups and the amount of time they have to spend in completing their studies. Now it is time for you to define how society will be able to recognize the achievement of your students (and teachers). What can you do? You will need to establish credentials certifying their achievements. You will award those credentials to students by assessing their performance. You will mandate to the rest of society these credentials as the one critical proof of achievement they can use to identify the utility or value of the student to their endeavors. These credentials will make their way to lists of minimal criteria for jobs, so students can find meaningful opportunities for their careers. Great institutions will implicitly add their own value and brand to the credentials, thereby enhancing their value for the rest of society. Over time, you may introduce new credentials or change the existing ones, in response to changing social or economic needs of your country or the world.

It is my strong belief that our system of education is not an industrial system that produces well-developed citizens; rather it is a system whose major output is to *industriously* generate credentials. All the work that children, teachers, school leaders, employers, and parents do is geared towards that one single goal – a goal that is unstated and obscured by visions of intentionally producing well-developed citizens.

It is not to state that it is the case of intentionality, and that there do not exist great examples of people and institutions that are not credential-hungry to the exclusion of higher order developmental goals. However, the fact remains that credentialing provides the bedrock on which the general system of education is based, and that largely determines how education and jobs are transacted in society.

You have seen and experienced this relatively global phenomenon. Whether it is standardized tests in the USA, exam boards in India, or the Gaokao in China, the struggle for marks and the need to compete for children and their parents is very visible. Parents realize that good scores are essential for forward mobility through the education system and critical for establishing the 'right' career options for their children. On the flip side, given that institutional capacity is low, selection is based on limited choice and fiercely competitive exams rather than advancing individual abilities, becomes the norm. The parameter for success becomes gaining entry into socially preferred choices such as engineering and medicine. As generally perceived, this also leads to a preponderance of rote learning and regurgitation. Popular film media has echoed some of this ethos with movies such as *Dead Poets Society*, *Good Will Hunting* and *3 Idiots*.[113]

Even if you do not share this belief, it is important to look closely at credentialing, insofar as it is an integral part of our system of education. Credentialing marks success in academics or professional skills. When interpreted correctly, it is a reflection of a student's ability. When interpreted wrongly, it has serious implications on our stated goals of fostering well-developed citizens.

## DESIGNING CREDENTIALS

How will you design such a system of credentialing? Imagine you are designing the exit points at each level of education. The exit points could be at each year of schooling, with particular emphasis on years which mark a transition from one part of the education system to the other. These exit points could mark the shift from academic to vocational streams, from studying all subjects to choosing a particular stream or track, specializing in a given discipline or choosing a professional skill development option. Your problem is quite complex. The system that you build has to be acceptable to all. It has to be objectively designed

113 Baxi, Viplav (2010). 3 Idiots: Educational Pedagogy or Fantasy, ***Viplav Baxi's Meanderings***, retrieved on November 26, 2017 from https://learnos.wordpress.com/2010/01/16/3-idiots-educational-pedagogy-or-fantasy/

with clear goals and a methodology geared for accuracy and credibility. It has to be easy to understand and adopt for practitioners, and with clear rules and training. You have to also choose your battles – handle every exam at every level and exit point or just focus on the important ones (like the end of term and school examinations). You have to ensure that the assessments are synchronized with the rest of the system – curricular goals, syllabi, methods, measures, evaluation system, school schedules, standardization, scoring methods and reporting. You have to be cognizant of individual differences across education boards, systems of education, certification agencies and many diverse collectives across the landscape. You have to be conscious of how and what you will assess, and why. You may also have the onerous task of standardizing the assessments since the results will need to be used as part of entry criteria throughout the country or even internationally. What are the options you have? How will you develop such a credentialing system? How will you design its implementation?

It is not an easy problem to solve without making gross assumptions about many things, including how learning happens. Typically, our educracy makes these assumptions starting from the definition of a credential to making its upstream connections with jobs and opportunities for higher and further education. It gives institutions legitimacy by conferring degree (one type of credentials) granting power on them. In return for that legitimacy and credibility, it demands conformance on other aspects such as curriculum and governance.

Let us define credentialing more broadly to include both formal and non-formal measures of achievement and other forms of recognition. The formal measures are generally based on institution-driven examinations and regular graded assessments, and entrance and exit exams such as those conducted for higher education and by specific education boards. These also include homework, projects and assignments which may or may not count towards the final grade. The informal measures are non-graded awards of some kind or the other, and also awards and recognition in other fields. Both measures contribute to building a picture of the student's capability, especially as it needs to be projected forward through the system.

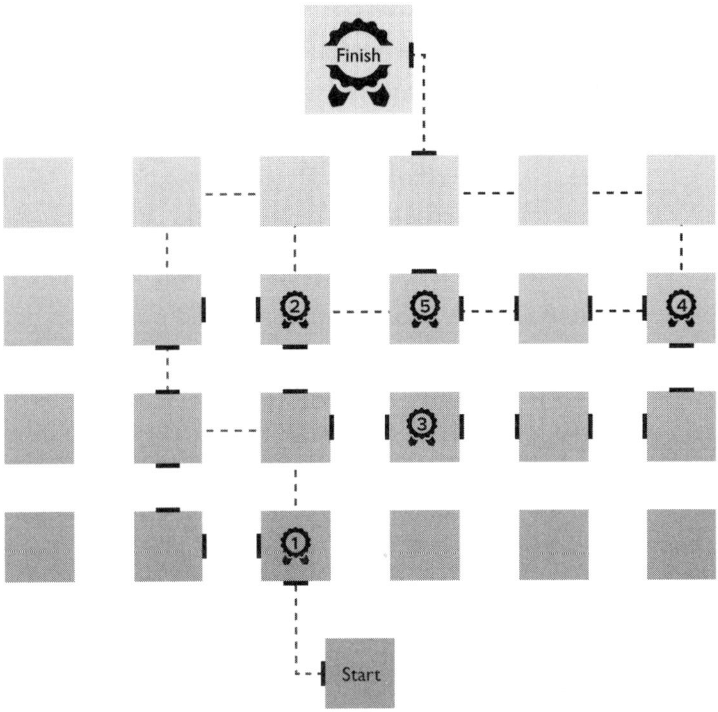


**Figure 12: The formal credentialing system**

Discussions around the formal measures are fraught with dissenting voices. Indian boards of education have, for the longest time (since 1992), followed a system of moderating marks. The reasons for moderating exam marks for the two crucial Board examinations in India (at the end of Class X and XII) are ostensibly to streamline the differences in subjectivity across examiners, moderate over the varying difficulty levels between sets of question papers for the same exam, allow students some grace for not having enough time to answer a difficult question and incredibly, to maintain pass parity across the years. This system is in a serious state of misuse, both statistically and philosophically:[114]

> The misuse was first highlighted in 2013 by two bloggers, Debarghya Das[115] and Prashant Bhattacharji[116,117], who mined board results of ICSE and CBSE respectively. Bhattacharji plotted the 2013 results on a graph that showed a sudden spike in the number of students scoring 95%. Das was able to demonstrate an oddly anomalous distribution of marks — for instance, not a single ICSE student that year had scored 81, 82, 84, 85, 87, 89, 91 or 92 in any subject.

Das and Bhattacharji showed a clear manipulation of marks by the country's two most venerated national boards of education. Most state-level boards in India have also shown this inflation of marks between the years 2004-16, perhaps to give their students an edge over other boards, in securing seats at prestigious higher education institutions across the country.

But even if marks are not moderated in this manner, is standardized testing still really effective? Is it really required? In the US, the furore over the spate of standardized testing that occurred after President Bush signed the No Child Left Behind Act in 2002, is increasing every year. The NCLB required children to be tested in Reading and Math from grades three to eight, and schools that could not demonstrate adequate progress were penalized. As a result, preparing for the tests became a major pre-occupation (and a costly one at that) to the exclusion of the

---

114 Chopra, Ritika (2017). No moderation, what real Class X and XII marks may mean, *The Indian Express*, May 5, 2017, retrieved on October 15, 2017 from http://indianexpress.com/article/explained/no-moderation-what-real-class-x-xii-marks-may-mean-4637897/

115 Das, Debarghya (2013). Hacking into the Indian education system, retrieved on October 15, 2017 from https://deedy.quora.com/Hacking-into-the-Indian-Education-System

116 Bhattacharji, Prashant (2013). Exposing CBSE and ICSE: statistical insights into the true lies on your marksheets, retrieved on October 15, 2017 from http://www.thelearningpoint.net/home/examination-results-2013/exposing-cbse-and-icse

117 Learningpoint.net (2013). A shocking story of marks tampering and inflation: data mining CBSE scoring for a decade, retrieved on April 30, 2019 from http://www.thelearningpoint.net/home/examination-results-2013/cbse-2004-to-2014-bulls-in-china-shops

development needs of children[118] and the professional development of teachers. A study by the American Federation of Teachers, 2013 showed that the proportion of test preparation time to the total learning time of students is quite significant (between 20-40 minutes each day in a 180-day schedule for one representative district, about 16 percent of total learning time).[119] At the same time, it was very clear that the tests mainly assessed the lower end of the skills, rather than higher-order thinking skills, which meant that a larger, crucial part of the learning time was not really spent for the right skills to be acquired.

In China, the National College Entrance Exam, the Gaokao, has attracted its fair share of criticism as well. The exam has been criticized for the high level of stress that it imposes on students. If you are in China at exam time, you will see professional 'nannies' (expert students who have passed the exam or under-graduates) apprentice aspirants, anxious parents boarding their child at a hotel near the test centre to save time, and taxis brandishing a yellow flag to demand the right of way for their test-taking passengers on the day of the exam.[120] Exam fraud is not uncommon with some parents paying large amounts for surrogate test taking. Advanced technology, including drones, is reportedly being deployed to prevent cheating.

When this kind of hysteria affects nearly 10 million students each year, it gains epidemic proportions. This hysteria is rationalized by an increasing number of institutions across the world accepting the Gaokao results in their entrance criteria (about a 1000 universities in 14 countries

---

118 Mulholland, Quinn (2015, May 14). The case against standardized testing, *Harvard Political Review*, retrieved on October 15, 2017 from http://harvardpolitics.com/united-states/case-standardized-testing/

119 Nelson, Howard (2013). Testing more, teaching less, What America's obsession with student testing costs in money and lost instructional time, American Federation of Teachers, retrieved on October 15, 2017 from http://www.aft.org/sites/default/files/news/testingmore2013.pdf

120 Tan, Yvette (2016, June 7). Gaokao season: China embarks on dreaded national exams, *BBC News*, retrieved on October 16, 2017 from http://www.bbc.com/news/world-asia-china-36457453

already accept these results), and by the Western academic fraternity acknowledging the strengths of the Chinese teaching methods and systems.[121,122]

This is not something limited to school education, but permeates higher and further education as well. There is a disproportionately higher degree of focus on assessments for the purpose of selection, and not enough on assessments for the purpose of advancing learning. In fact, the importance ascribed to these assessments leads to a dominance of rote learning in the system, while the need of the hour is to focus on deeper learning.[123]

## INFORMAL CREDENTIALS

The more informal measures have been around for a long time. These have spanned both academic and non-academic activities. Earlier physical badges, certificates, and 'good chits' were handled offline. With the invention of digital badges and the growing Open Badges movement over the past decade or so, students and candidates have been able to display their skills and achievements on the web as part of their portfolio and credentials. Certifiers have used digital badges to provide verified credentials. More than scores or marks, these badges have become widely accepted. In some cases, Blockchain[124] technologies have been implemented for maintaining a secure online ledger for formal and informal credentials.

---

121 Gu, Mini (2016, May 2). The Gaokao: History, reform, and rising international significance of China's National College Entrance Examination, *WENR*, retrieved on April 30, 2019 from https://wenr.wes.org/2016/05/the-gaokao-history-reform-and-international-significance-of-chinas-national-college-entrance-examination

122 Ash, Alec (2016, October 12). Is China's Gaokao the world's toughest school exam?, *The Guardian*, retrieved on October 16, 2017 from https://www.theguardian.com/world/2016/oct/12/gaokao-china-toughest-school-exam-in-world

123 Tower, Luke (2014, November 25). Deeper learning: moving students beyond memorization, *NEAToday,* retrieved on October 16, 2017 from http://neatoday.org/2014/11/25/deeper-learning-moving-students-beyond-memorization-2/

124 Russell, Jon (2017, August 9). Sony wants to digitize education records using the blockchain, *Techcrunch*, retrieved on October 16, 2017 from https://techcrunch.com/2017/08/09/sony-education-blockchain/

as expert co-learners rather than as instructors. The sheer diversity in the community created tremendously exciting opportunities for learning.

CCK08 also illustrated four key principles of MOOCs – diversity, autonomy, openness, and interactivity. Diversity is reflected in the contributions that people make, leveraging their own perspectives, to the wider network. Autonomy is critical for learners to evaluate choices, ideas and perspectives according to their own needs and goals. Openness is important to ensure that every person is able to move in and out of the learning experience, without impeding boundaries. Interactivity is important from the perspective of learning to 'be' a reflective practitioner as opposed to learning to 'know'. To participate in a MOOC then, would be to engage in a democratic learning experience.[249]

As a result learning 'emerged' rather than being pre-designed. Participants learnt to be practitioners rather than just 'learning to know' or even 'learning to do'. CCK08 also redefined the roles of teachers and students. The role of the teacher as an expert learner was to *model and demonstrate* while the learner had to *practice and reflect.*

Such a learning ecosystem reflects the reality of learning in a digital age, where information is over- abundant, knowledge is increasingly specialized, change is extremely rapid, networks and social media have revolutionized communication, and learning has become largely informal. Such systems of learning can potentially solve the burning problem of employability of our students. It can help them gain the capability to become lifelong learners, acquire 21$^{st}$ century skills and effectively negotiate the rapid shifts in the nature of work. It can raise the quality of teaching and learning significantly, in an equitable and affordable manner.

This thinking is also reflected in the concept of heutagogy – the study of self-determined learning – that, unlike pedagogy and andragogy, marks

---

249 Downes, Stephen (2010, October 22). What is democracy in education, *Half an Hour*, retrieved on November 13, 2017 from http://www.downes.ca/post/54025

a significant move away from traditional teacher-centered learning. Heutagogy extends the popular theory of andragogy or self-directed learning by focusing on 'capability.' Capable people are those who 'know how to learn; are creative; have a high degree of self-efficacy; can apply competencies in novel as well as familiar situations; and can work well with others.'[250]

Since 2008, there have been a large number of MOOCs on the lines of CCK08. These MOOCs such as the *Future of Education*, *Critical Literacies*, *Change 11* and other versions of CCK itself, have seen rich interaction globally. A lot of published research and a strong community of educators, theorists, developers and thought-leaders have emerged. There have been critics too.[251] They questioned whether Connectivism could be rightfully called a theory of learning or if it was just a combination of many ideas put together in an instructional framework intended to guide teaching and learning in a digital age. Downes[252] and Siemens have argued that it presents an altogether new vocabulary to describe learning and stands up as a theory in its own right. It isn't a debate that has decisive answers for now.

## RHIZOMATIC LEARNING

Cormier evolved the concept of Rhizomatic Learning[253] on the basis of which he has grown the Rhizo-MOOC.

---

250 Hase, Stewart and Chris Kenyon, (2000). From Andragogy to Heutagogy, retrieved on April 30, 2019 from http://pandora.nla.gov.au/nph-wb/20010220130000/http://ultibase.rmit.edu.au/Articles/dec00/hase2.htm

251 Wade, M.C. (2012, May 30). A critique of connectivism as a learning theory, *cybergouge*, retrieved on November 12, 2017 from http://cybergogue.blogspot.in/2012/05/critique-of-connectivism-as-learning.html

252 Downes, Stephen (2014, April 21). Connectivism as learning theory, *Half an Hour*, retrieved on November 12, 2017 from http://halfanhour.blogspot.in/2014/04/connectivism-as-learning-theory.html

253 Cormier, Dave (2008, June 3). Rhizomatic education: community as curriculum, retrieved on November 12, 2017 from http://davecormier.com/edblog/2008/06/03/rhizomatic-education-community-as-curriculum/

> A rhizomatic plant has no center and no defined boundary; rather, it is made up of a number of semi-independent nodes, each of which is capable of growing and spreading on its own, bounded only by the limits of its habitat.

Cormier described a learning experience similar to a rhizome wherein learning itself is organic and emergent, deeply driven by personal context, flexible boundaries, and multiple pathways. Rhizomatic teaching, in turn, describes a teaching experience that sets the context, facilitates the inter-connections of ideas through conversations, and empowers the community to engineer its own curriculum.

Rhizomatic Learning builds up the core capability to learn in a distributed learning environment. It leverages all the attendant benefits of network-led and community-based learning, but distinguishes itself by describing a personal 'self-reproducing' capability to learn. The agency to learn rests with the learner and the learning community she is part of. The agency to teach is distributed among all the learners, who really establish the curriculum. The resultant is messy and complex, with individual outcomes possibly far in deviation to any expected outcomes from the community.

In Rhizomatic Learning, the definition of a course veers away from the traditional. It is a sense of time-bound evented-ness, a shared context which aggregates a community. Its curriculum is formed by the community, which evolves and extends it continuously through prior knowledge and emergent opinions. It may engender several artistic and creative forms of expression, not necessarily formal artifacts associated with traditional courses.

Rhizomatic Learning is characterized by *learning freedom*. It draws heavily upon openness, lack of centralized control, autonomy, diversity and interaction. Freedom in learning drives most of the interactions, liberating the learning experience.

In contrast, connectivist models uphold 'connection-making' as the primary source of learning and knowledge. There is connection-making in Rhizomatic Learning, but that is merely a medium. The focus is on free, unrestricted sharing and unpredictable pathways in learning. In that sense, the *afterthought* focus on *Critical Literacies*[254] in the connectivist MOOCs, becomes the starting point for Rhizomatic Learning. What is 'tidy' in the network model, becomes messy in the rhizomatic one. The replication of learning capability in distributed environments is key – the 'more of how you can learn, is learning' of Rhizomatic Learning overwhelms the 'those that have, get' rules of networks. In that sense, Rhizomatic Learning deliberately empowers personalized learning.

## xMOOCS AND cMOOCS

The MOOCs as originally envisioned, meant questioning the existing paradigm from the perspective of a digital age, scale, and effectiveness. Downes puts it succinctly when he says:[255]

> MOOCs were not designed to serve the missions of the elite colleges and universities. They were designed to undermine them, and make those missions obsolete. Yes there has been a great rebranding and co-option of the concept of the MOOC over the last couple of years. The near-instant response from the elites, almost unprecedented in my experience, is a recognition of the deeply subversive intent and design of the original MOOCs (which they would like very much to erase from history).

254 Downes, Stephen (2015, October 30). Critical literacies and the challenge of online learning, retrieved on November 13, 2017 from http://www.downes.ca/presentation/369; The Critical Literacies MOOC investigated the literacies we need to have in a digital learning environment. See also Steve Mackenzie - http://learnadoodledastic.blogspot.in/2010/06/critical-literacy-course-online.html

255 Downes, Stephen (2013, April 13). The great rebranding, *Half an Hour,* retrieved on November 12, 2017 from http://halfanhour.blogspot.in/2013/04/the-great-rebranding.html

Siemens summarized his interpretation of the difference between the original MOOCs and the new ones by stating,[256] '...there is overlap between our model and that of *Coursera/EDx*. However, *Coursera/EDx* emulates the existing education system, choosing instead to *transfer* it online rather than *transform* it online'.

To distinguish between the two, Downes termed the original MOOCs 'cMOOCs' (for Connectivist MOOCs) and the newer ones as 'xMOOCs', the 'x' standing for being an extension of something else. That something else was really the type of eLearning that had grown very rapidly since the late 1990s. Corporations and even online learning providers found it expedient to digitize expensive face to face training and create standardized, mass learning experiences for their employees, in order to cut costs and save working time that was lost in training and travel.

Siemens also distinguishes further between these two. He makes the point that in cMOOCs, coherence is 'learner formed and instructor guided.' Learners make sense and find their way through the interactions in a network. At times they synchronize or harmonize, not solely to the demands of the instructor, but also with learners and the state of 'knowledge' in the network. In the xMOOCs, however, instructors are at the core, the curriculum mercilessly harmonizes instruction, and learners operate in narrow groups rather than as connective networks or communities of practice.

For the most part, the xMOOCs tried to simply replicate the traditional classroom and curricular practices online. In traditional online learning, all learning is centrally directed, restricted to the closed boundaries of the course, performed generally alone (collaboration features exhibit very low usage patterns), mass personalized with rigid pre-determined learning paths and assessed largely through objective type assessments.

---

256 Siemens, George (2012, June 6). What is the theory that underpins our MOOCs, retrieved on 22 July, 2018 from http://www.elearnspace.org/blog/2012/06/03/what-is-the-theory-that-underpins-our-moocs/

This type of eLearning had already failed to scale for many reasons. It was designed for stereotypes of industrial age learners. It ignored the diversity and overabundance of information that is present in real life. It ignored the autonomy of learners who needed to personalize the learning experience. It ignored the richness of interaction on the World Wide Web. It did not empower learners with the agency and choice it needed in setting the curricular agenda. It ignored the 'conversation' and 'connections' in learning. xMOOCs are extensions of this type of eLearning.

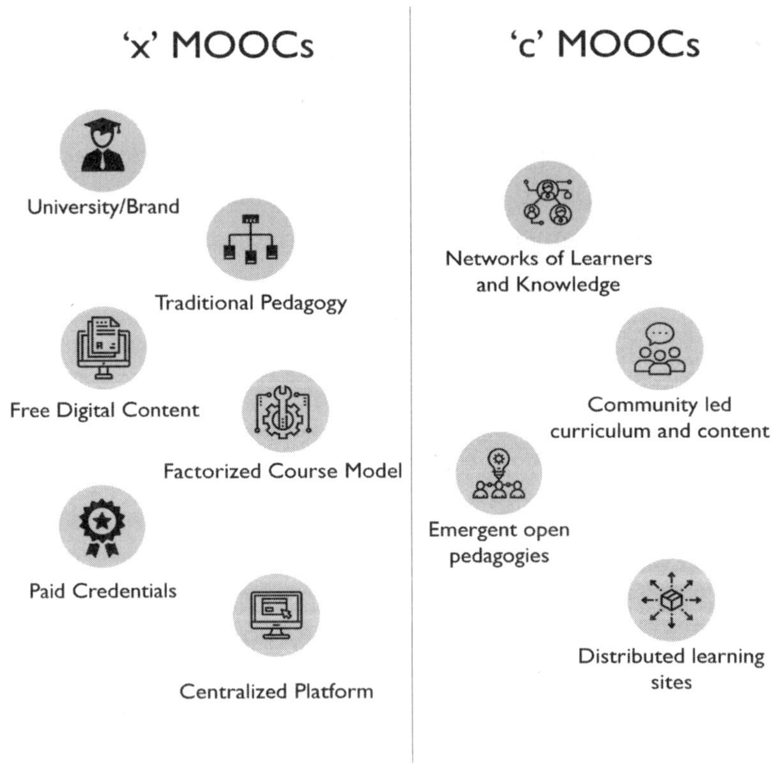


**Figure 23: Distinguishing between xMOOCs and cMOOCs**

By only incrementally extending this type of online learning, xMOOCs have massively magnified challenges such as low retention, rote learning, low employability, and lack of student ownership, motivation, interactivity, and engagement. It is as if they have ignored more than two decades of insights from online, open, and distance education.

There are two key challenges facing the xMOOCs. First, the pedagogy behind these xMOOCs needs a rethink. They have adopted the title MOOC but ignored the rich underlying connectivist origins. They have merely extended traditional online, instructivist Web Based Training (WBT) and Instructor Led Training (ILT) methods to a massive audience.

WBTs and ILTs were designed as eLearning equivalents, of expensive classroom training, to reduce training delivery costs and standardize instruction for large scale corporate training. But nearly everyone realizes that this type of eLearning is not scalable because it is designed for learner stereotypes, does not account for real world diversity and in general, predates and ignores the entire social learning revolution. A WBT is usually to be consumed in an isolated self-paced manner and is directed at a specific perception of who the target of this mass produced course is.

Both for WBTs/ILTs and xMOOCs, the model is largely teacher (and/or instructional designer) led and content-driven. It not based upon socially negotiated, digitally mediated and distributed learning, the hallmark of the cMOOCs. This is why it is perhaps more appropriate to call them XBTs (or 'massive' extensions of WBTs and ILTs) rather than think of them as a variant of the original MOOC approach.

The XBTs augment the traditional systems, giving importance to institutional pedigree, clearly defined institutional structures and processes (such as courses, terms and exams) and certification mechanisms. XBTs are closed, insular micro-systems of learning, replicating the scholastic structure of the classroom and the administrative structure of the qualification or degree, to an approximate online form.

The connectivist MOOCs are very open, emphasize sense-making, operate in a distributed fashion, legitimize learners at the periphery (legitimate peripheral participation or 'lurking') and do not impose the strict conformance to traditional notions of course, exam, and certification. For them, since learning is the process of making connections and knowledge is the network, the competency and capability to learn, critically determines the learning itself.

The cMOOC platforms enable the conversation by aggregating the member contributions, making them accessible by remixing and repurposing them in forms that are useful to search/consume and feeding them forward to members. This mechanism results in the course progressing into areas not anticipated when the cMOOC was conceptualized. In this sense, learning becomes an emergent phenomenon with ever changing contours. And learners learn to adapt to these dynamic conditions and to self-organize in ways that are meaningful to them. This is what happens in real life as we learn and evolve. This is not very helpful as a design for replication for planners who, as you could well imagine, cannot operate in such apparently dynamic environments.

Secondly, engagement and retention are key aspects of the learning experience that the MOOCs, in general, have not been able to address effectively. The long tail of learning, which is that a really large number of learners end up not completing the MOOC or remain at low levels of engagement, is nothing new. It is just that the massive nature of MOOCs amplifies some of these known issues.

It is here that the MOOC providers need to spend a lot of time experimenting with techniques such as gamification, badges, adaptive learning, and learning analytics. At scale, many new ways of analyzing and predicting the behavior of networked learners, have emerged. Analysis of learning 'trails' or records of learner behavior over time, can help predict, for example, students at-risk of failure. They can help educators and learners equally through actionable insights.

conceived at the time of creating the first design. Over time, the weaver must also enrich the design with her own and her learners' evolution in the network in a seamless way.

Educators can also be viewed as pattern builders – those who are able to build logical interconnections to make a field intelligible to the learner at each stage of learning. The educator must preserve the patterns in a way that can be accessed and re-harnessed for future reference and for new learners. This is a critical function. In the existing paradigm, many great learning experiences are simply lost because the people that enable these experiences leave the system without recording them. There must be a framework that can allow related patterns (Paris is the capital of France vs Paris is where Disneyland is), to accumulate. This accumulation also needs to have temporal and other annotations that the educator can describe to make patterns far more discoverable. The skill involved would be akin to building a discovery and recommendation service such as the ones Amazon or Google have built, over time leveraging the advances in machine learning and Big Data.

The skills of educators in deciphering progress through networks are vastly different from the ways they currently know and understand. At the core of it is determining the degree of connectedness of students to relevant networks of people and resources – an evaluation of their own PLNs. Immediately after that is the assessment of practices when they are interacting with others in those networks, how they are able to harness information and then make sense of it. This also includes assessments of the quality of interactions within their PLNs. Traditional tools of assessment are no longer very relevant in this scenario. New measures of the degree of connectedness and the quality of interactions then need to underpin assessment rubrics.

## NEW AGE SKILLS

All these different conceptions of the roles of educators, point to different skills that they may need or want to attain. This prompts us to question why we should expect all teachers to learn the same or similar skills, while at the same time providing richly differentiated career and interest options for children. Can't there be new and diverse types of career profiles and options created for teachers? For example, what if teachers could get training to be professional coaches, experiential educators, assessment experts, psychometric, *edTech* or analytics gurus, and so on? What if a teacher could also become the school CTO or its Chief Data Scientist or its Chief Learning Officer? Are these roles even real? Today, we have broad strokes with which we 'paint' all educators – academic vs. a physical education teacher, primary vs. secondary or tertiary, teacher vs. a headmaster, a headmaster vs. a district or government official, and so on. But these may not be the only specializations that we may want our teachers to attain. And these may not be the only roles they play.

Let us take for example the role of educators as data scientists. It is certainly true that there are many people promising machine learning as the end-game for teaching-learning at one end, and equally many people who mistrust over-reliance on data and 'teaching machines' citing serious privacy concerns and a preference for intuition and personal touch at the other end. But it is also equally important to appreciate that unless the educators actively experiment with data and machine learning in the form and with the intent they choose, we will never really find out whether it could be applied at scale.[147] It is not just that – intelligent systems are already becoming what search accomplished for the early worldwide web – and a future without intelligent computing in every walk of life is inconceivable now. So there is an urgent need for educators to make their presence felt in this new ecosystem.

147 Stone, Adam (2017, June 2). Will data scientists have a big impact in education?, Centre for Digital Education, retrieved on October 22, 2017 from http://www.centerdigitaled.com/k-12/Will-Data-Scientists-Have-a-Big-Impact-on-Education.html

**Figure 15: Emerging roles that teachers can play**

To understand a bit more about what educators could do with this new and promising area of research, we need educators trained in it and education researchers to focus on harnessing all this fast improving computing power and intelligence for solving problems that we face today. One of the areas of global interest is in aiding teachers to handle multi-grade multi-level classrooms. All classrooms have mixed abilities, but many classrooms are also multi-grade (such as in remote rural locations with low infrastructure). For such classrooms, there is a potential for teachers to encourage self-learning, track and act on the data so generated and improve interaction effectiveness. Even for classrooms that are not multi-grade, under certain conditions, intelligent learning environments can help students of varying abilities to navigate the syllabus more effectively.

Experiential education is another skill that could well turn out to be a specialization in itself. One look at Andrew Vanden Heuvel's expedition to CERN[148] is enough to understand the possibilities. Andrew is a Physics Teacher from a school in Michigan. He decided to try out Google Glass, a special eyewear product from Google that had an embedded computer and camera built into it. Using Glass, he decided to take his

148 Explorer Story: Andrew Vanden Heuvel through Google Glass, retrieved on October 22, 2017 from https://www.youtube.com/watch?v=VGoL9PWB0s4

brother's class on a virtual expedition to CERN in Switzerland. While at CERN, Andrew connected to the class and all the students could not only see the insides of the large Hadron collider, but also interact with local staff, ask questions and see things operating. It was an educational experience mediated by Andrew to a class of students thousands of miles away. It was a more real experience than the (current) virtual reality experiences, at least in terms of the interaction quality itself.

If children from classrooms everywhere, and not just students for whom access to specialist educators like Andrew is the only choice, could connect in such experiential ways with one another, local insights and support for negotiating a diverse curriculum could be integrated into mainstream education.

Another area of great potential is the Internet of Things – a way to connect millions of devices over the Internet in a simple and affordable manner. For example, the Birmingham Urban Climate Laboratory invites schools to join projects that leverage a large network of devices for measuring temperature, precipitation, relative humidity, wind speed and direction, pressure and solar radiation.[149] Students can study weather patterns and perform a wide variety of analytics on the data received from these sensors. The feeling they are dealing with something live around them that they can experience, helps students contextualize their learning. The potential is amazing – the entire world could (theoretically) be one giant experiential lab for learning. If educators could actively experiment with such technological affordances, it is possible that some important challenges in the system may be addressed very effectively. But today, there is a lack of specialization in Experiential Education that we would do well to address a role that perhaps a Chief Experience Officer at the school could play.

---

149 High Density Measurements within the Urban Environment, retrieved on October 22, 2017 from https://www.birmingham.ac.uk/schools/gees/centres/bucl/hitemp/index.aspx

The role of an educator in protecting privacy and confidential information of their students and their activities at school is extremely important. With the fast growing use of the Internet for educational purposes and the introduction of multiple software, hardware and services from partners, it is increasing becoming critical for schools to understand their responsibility in the information chain. They need skilled educators who understand both new media and networks and also the teaching and learning process.

With every new role new challenges will come that educators will need to navigate. The biggest challenge for educators will perhaps be to first redefine their roles and then acquire new skills to help them meet the challenges of those new roles in the not so distant future. What will it be for you?

# #8

# What*If*

## teachers played games with students?

# #8 WHAT*IF* TEACHERS PLAYED GAMES WITH STUDENTS?

*Games and simulations form a core part of how students interact with technology today. What if teachers were to become part of that ecosystem of play? What if they challenged students from within their own contexts of play?*

*What if they used that ecosystem to drive learning outcomes? What if they gained greater insight into student attitudes, behaviors and skills through an assessment of their gameplay? What if they encouraged their grit, passion, and commitment to overcome challenges? What if they employed gameplay to make their own learning joyful and fun?*

When this question was first posted online as part of the **WhatIfEDU** series, a reader made an almost instant comment - '*they would lose!*'

As an educator, you may either see games as distractions or as a powerful tool to enhance learning. Opinions are sharply divided. It is still an esoteric field. You may feel that games are for play not for learning. You may not be convinced that some games could have serious educational value. Even if you are, you may be hard pressed to find the right game for your class. And then even if you did find the right game, you may never be able to convince your school to add the results of game performance to the annual report card. But if you have been able to do all this, then you have probably found that games have led to increased student engagement and performance, and perhaps you would like to make them a regular feature in your classroom.

## GAMES, GAMIFICATION, AND SIMULATIONS

Games, simulations, and gamification are not alien concepts for teachers. Many teachers do use games or game-play (gamification) as a method for increasing class engagement or when dealing with specific curricular needs (when these employ serious games or simulations). But the vision of a teacher playing Candy Crush or the World of Warcraft with her students is not widely encountered, except in certain specialized programs such as Microsoft's Minecraft in Education, or staple MBA program games and simulations like those for stock markets and strategic decision making. It is also not certain that teachers and parents will find value in and allow student engagement with popular genres of entertainment games or even consider them useful in an educational context. Perhaps more people than not view them as distractions they must keep children away from.

A game is basically characterized by three things – objectives and goals that the player must accomplish, the rules and tools of the game, and increasing levels of achievement and complexity. For example, the addition of two numbers when played like a game has the goal of addition, the rules that addition conforms to, tools and techniques such as mental or Vedic mathematics and levels of complexity ranging from single digit numbers to complex term configurations including fractions, negative numbers, and the like. In terms of presentation, the game may involve a simple display of the mathematical expression on the screen, with the player having to evaluate the answer, or a complex visual scenario where completing a fictional task requires the player to evaluate an expression in order to proceed further. Time is an important component of the rules of the game. So is the number of players – one or more – and their level of cooperation in the game.

Game designers often constrain the amount of time available to make a decision or judgment and increase the rewards if the user completes certain activities or steps within a certain threshold of time for the task. Sometimes the game may also personalize to the level of the player, but typically the rules are consistent. Accomplishment is a standardized measure in most games. The levels completed and the rewards obtained are something to talk about and share widely for players. In fact, gamer reputation is built on their prowess at playing the game (shown through leaderboards that display player rankings).

Typically, each level of accomplishment unlocks the next level of tasks and upgrades the status of the players such that they become more powerful in the game itself by gaining special privileges. The reward system is usually designed to sustain and increase motivation levels – tasks may not be too difficult to start with and the rewards higher for accomplishing the first few tasks, but then it could get progressively more difficult to be rewarded as the game progresses. In fact, some games have cheat codes that allow them to unlock a higher level or complete a task if stuck, and this is an important progress mechanism.

Games can also be multi-player games in which two or more players or teams collaborate and compete. This allows teamwork and intuition to be developed over time and places additional demands on players to evaluate their playing style and the level of coordination with other players. Games may be played in various contexts and may be online/offline, physical or device based, 2D or 3D/virtual, motion-aware or location-aware and accompanied by many frills, such as sound and visual effects that add to the game play and player motivation.

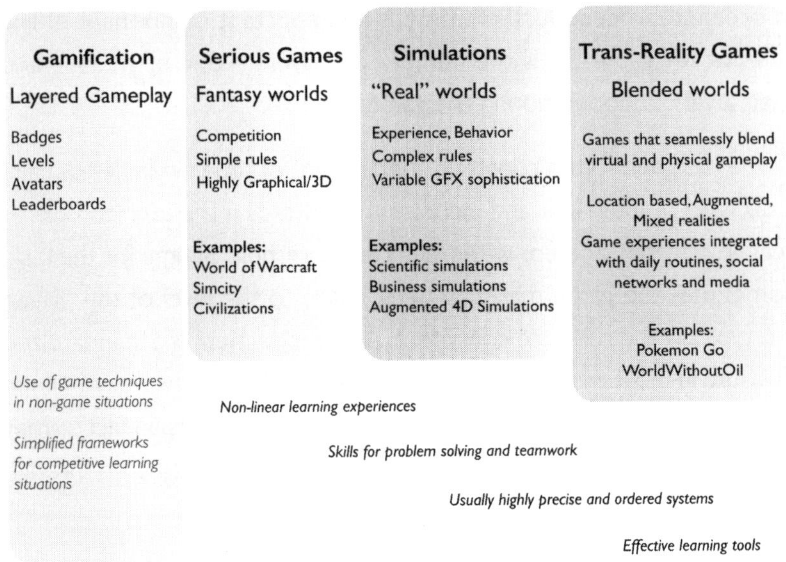


**Figure 16: A taxonomy of gamification, serious games and simulations**

Games are played for entertainment as well as serious purposes. When used for a serious purpose, they are called serious games. One of the serious purposes considered by game designers is formal education, but education is not the only use of serious games. Some serious games build productivity, some focus on compliance to processes in a corporate or industrial setting, and there can be many other intended uses in sectors like healthcare and defense. But the core mechanics of the game concern the task or challenge, the rules and the levels of complexity with an associated reward system.

Are there any benefits to gameplay? Are there valid fears that games are distractions? The benefits and issues with game play are well documented. At one end, games can offer tremendous value for players, increasing cognitive, psychomotor, and even emotional (affective) abilities and skills. At the other end, they can also become chronic obsessions with serious mental and physical consequences. But with proper and guided use, games can and should be used in a variety of contexts by teachers and learners.

A partial approach to gaming is called *gamification.* It involves the use of game techniques in typically non-game scenarios. This could be a company encouraging hackers to spot security bugs or a loyalty program that builds engagement with the brand, it could equally be a teacher in a classroom using game elements in some way (like a timed quiz which has a competitive element) to increase engagement when teaching, say, the human anatomy, or classification of animals and plants. Being less rigorous than games, gamification techniques are also more transient and less intensive on time and effort. This makes them suitable to be employed in a wide variety of situations.

Gamification is also usually the most common technique employed by digital content creators. They would typically take a format like 'Jeopardy' or 'Who wants to be a Millionaire' and use the same principles to 'gamify' a learning task. The learning task itself could be, for example, a quiz or a sorting exercise, which is not exactly fun delivered as-is. The gameplay element adds a certain level of engagement and motivates students to complete the learning task.

While games usually deal with fictional contexts and gamification with overlays of game techniques on real world situations, simulations directly deal with well-defined real world contexts. Examples include a flight simulator, a marine operations simulator or a medical training simulator; but also may include real-world modeling of (say) science experiments at school. Being embedded in the real world, simulators offer a direct application of concepts learnt, a fail-safe environment for practice and almost 'real' outcomes based on decisions taken. The 'fail-safe' nature of simulations and games is critical in most serious contexts, although there are inglorious instances where these conditions may be violated and the safety of players compromised. It is critical because it provides space for experimentation with little or no real world consequences, encouraging learning by doing and remedying mistakes through a real time feedback system.

I once heard or read about a history teacher in a remote corner of India, who decided she was going to take her students on an archaeology expedition. All she did to immerse her students in learning to be archaeologists was to actually create a 'heritage' site on campus. She dug a hole in the school grounds, buried a lot of artifacts that resembled those that could have come from that age in history that she was teaching, and then got her students to spend the day digging and excavating the site. Each discovery must have been quite a sight! That teacher demonstrated the power of simulation and she did it with her local resources and ingenuity. But it is more common to find technology enabled simulations that model situations difficult to recreate in real-life, and to sometimes go beyond it to set up fictional contexts.

A worthy example is alternate reality games. In a global serious game built around a fictional oil crisis,[150] called a *World Without Oil*, participants tried to 'live' through the first 32 weeks of a world suddenly facing a severe oil shortage. Participants started real discussions, conducted real interviews, and debated on how to handle the crisis. Through a citizen crisis nerve center, the simulation designers aggregated real time news

---

150 A World Without Oil, About, retrieved on December 2, 2017 from http://writerguy.com/wwo/metaabout.htm

and views, bringing fresh new information into the debate. It was like it was actually happening, and people were experiencing the emotions they would have experienced if it was real. The participants came up with their own solutions such as 'acts that mould communities, slash wasteful consumption, and create more "elastic" lives'. The game had a profound impact on the lives and attitudes of the participants.

Games, gamification, and simulations are interchangeably understood and interpreted, but there are key differences between these that educators should note. These 'instruments', when used in serious contexts can lend themselves to building capability and important skills in students and teachers. This 'learning with play' has many benefits. It increases motivation and engagement, builds skills such as problem solving and critical thinking, encourages collaboration and promotes experimentation.

## PLAY AS A SERIOUS TOOL

Play is a vital tool for both the teacher and the student, and more educators and parents need to embrace play as part of the learning and teaching process. It can solve many existing issues, such as the preponderance of rote learning and teaching, lack of development of skills and engagement, motivation and commitment to learning. But it is also widely misunderstood to be a distraction, rather than an aid to teaching and learning.

This misunderstanding basically stems from genuine concerns around real world transference – how can games encourage the development of skills in tangible and measurable ways, suited to the current systems of education? For example, can we expect scores from a game like *Candy Crush* to be on school report cards? Let us see if that even makes sense.

Game educators at *LearningWorks for Kids* have this description of the game.[151]

151 LearningWorks for Kids, retrieved on October 26, 2017 from http://learningworksforkids.com/playbooks/candy-crush-saga/

> *Candy Crush* saga is a puzzle game that involves making matches of three or more colored candy pieces. Players swap candy pieces either horizontally and vertically, and once a match is made, the candy disappears, causing the surrounding pieces of candy to fall into the empty spaces. This sometimes causes a chain reaction, netting players bonuses in the form of increased score and power-ups. The game also tosses in obstacles for players, like covering candy in jelly that must be eliminated before the candy can be matched. There are more than 100 levels of gameplay, with five different game modes that mix up the goals and maps of the levels so that there is always a fresh challenge. The game is easy to learn and play, but quite a challenge to fully master. Players can take on the saga by themselves, or they may connect with *Facebook* users to play against others to test their skills and see who can dominate the leaderboard. *Candy Crush* saga is appropriate for and playable by kids as young as five years old, although they may experience difficultly passing some of the deeper and more advanced levels of the game.

*Candy Crush* builds certain competencies in the players. The first set of competencies involves cognition. Children learn to recognize patterns, visualize new formations, solve problems, strategize and make judgments. The second set of competencies involves the psychomotor or kinesthetic domain, where they are physically engaged in the game and build reflexes, fine motor skills, and speed. The third set of competencies is around the affective or emotional domain, where they learn goal-setting, grit, time management, competition and collaboration. The fourth set of competencies is around metacognition – reflecting upon their learning – where they learn to improve upon their last performance, gain tips from more experienced players and find holes through the system to perform better. Game mechanisms such as spiraling ('chain') rewards, levels of complexity, leaderboards and engaging themes and designs, are experienced by the child as she plays the game. Learning the ropes at one game level allows a steeper learning curve for the other levels she plays.

These are skills we generally talk about building in the classroom. These are taxonomies of skills that teachers use to create traditional content and assessments. The real differences between a classroom game, or a game for a serious purpose, and a game played for entertainment, lie in the context, application and desired outcomes.

If a game can really build these skills in a virtual and disconnected (from the classroom) manner, how do we leverage those skills in the classroom so that the student can perform better? In this example, teachers could embed gameplay as homework ('homeplay'), play related problems in class and assess progress through the game and through application of skills learnt in the game to topics taught in class.

Of particular importance is one of the skills not usually measured in school – grit. Angela Duckworth's work on grit[152] and its impact on learning shows that 'grit, a combination of passion and perseverance for a singularly important goal—is the hallmark of high achievers in every domain'. In particular, games are all about building grit because they are inherently designed to present ever higher levels of challenges to achieve a specific goal.

In fact, game design principles can also provide educators instructional design tips[153] – how to design their teaching so that it creates similar effects – such as 'chunking content into episodes and levels, clearly communicated and measurable objectives, hints and shuffles to keep the game moving, limitless opportunity to repeat levels, bonuses for surpassing acceptable performance, immediate feedback, scaffolds, built-in choices for students, relieving the stress of the formal exam or quiz and

152 Duckworth, Angela (2016). Grit, *the power of passion and perseverance*, retrieved on December 2, 2017 from http://angeladuckworth.com/grit-book/

153 Varonis, Evangeline Marlos and Varonis, Evangeline, Maria (2015). Deconstructing candy crush: What instructional design can learn from game design, *The International Journal of Information and Learning Technology*, Vol. 32 ( 3) pp. 150 – 164, retrieved on August 5, 2018 from https://www.researchgate.net/publication/277906158_Deconstructing_Candy_Crush_what_instructional_design_can_learn_from_game_design

much more.'[154] The interplay of games and classroom instruction is not fixed, rather it evolves as more people play the game and engage in the classroom. The diversity leads to ever-increasing self-awareness, such that children find it easier to learn and advance through the learning, replicating prior sets of learning through active reflection.

The fact that there is real world transference of skills through play is supported by theory as well as empirical evidence. Stephen Gillett, who was earlier the very young Chief Information Officer at Starbucks, put his game experience on his resume.[155] The game he played was the *World of Warcraft* (WoW), a massively multi-player online game played by tens of millions of people worldwide.

On the outside, nothing could sound more incongruous with his work profile than the story[156] of the game itself.

> For ages, the fallen titan Sargeras plotted to scour all life from Azeroth. To this end, Sargeras possessed the human sorcerer Medivh and compelled him to contact Gul'dan, an orc warlock on the world of Draenor. There, Sargeras' demonic servants among the Burning Legion worked to corrupt the once - peaceful orcs and forge them into a bloodthirsty army known as the Horde. This cursed force invaded Azeroth through the Dark Portal, a dimensional gateway created by Medivh and Gul'dan, and clashed with the human nation of Stormwind. Aided by the half-orc Garona, human champions like Anduin Lothar fought valiantly to protect their kingdom. Yet, in the end, the mighty Horde shattered Stormwind's defenses. Amid the city's tragic fall, Garona betrayed her allies and assassinated King Llane Wrynn, sealing the nation's defeat.

---

154 Varonis, Evangeline Marlos and Varonis, Evangeline, Maria (2015). ***Designing an Academic Course? Five Tips from candy crush that you need to know***, Emerald publishing, retrieved on October 28, 2017 from http://www.emeraldgrouppublishing.com/promo/crush_info.htm

155 Pagliery, Jose (2014, June 19). Why I put World of Warcraft on my resume, ***CNNtech,*** retrieved on October 28, 2017 from http://money.cnn.com/2014/06/19/technology/world-of-warcraft-resume/index.html

156 Warcraft: Orcs and Humans, retrieved on October 28, 2017 from https://worldofwarcraft.com/en-us/story/timeline

However, WoW helped build some key skills for Gillett that were necessary for his job as a CIO at one of the world's leading companies.

> Gillett said he includes his *World of Warcraft* achievements on his resume, because it's not just about role-playing games. It shows he exercises leadership in both the physical and virtual realms. Plus, he understands the current societal fascination with earning points and interactive entertainment.

Gillett ended up gamifying customer experience at Starbucks, by designing a very successful customer loyalty initiative. Later, he moved to Symantec, a cyber-security and antivirus company, and worked on games and simulators in the hiring process, and for customers to report bugs or errors in the software. What is really crucial is that not only did the skills of leadership, creativity, team management, recruitment, critical thinking and teamwork built playing WoW help him in landing these impressive jobs, but also that the skills learnt while playing could be adapted and applied to many extremely different contexts – after all, Starbucks and Symantec are extremely different businesses, operating in different ways and with widely different products (unless you can think of virus-scanning your coffee before you drink it).

A similar experience is narrated by Nicholas Cole.[157] At 17, he was one of the highest ranked Warcraft players in the world.

> Couldn't tell you a single thing I learned in math class between 1st grade and 12th grade, but I can tell you exactly how to arbitrage Linen Cloth on the Auction House to make a fortune….I have connected with an astounding number of entrepreneurs who attribute their success in entrepreneurship to their early gaming days…Only us gamers realize leading 40 raiders through a dungeon and leading a company utilizes very similar skill sets.

157 Cole, Nicholas (2017). 10 ways the world of warcraft is identical to the world of entrepreneurship, *INC*, retrieved on October 28, 2017 from https://www.inc.com/nicolas-cole/10-ways-world-of-warcraft-is-identical-to-world-of-entrepreneurship.html

## GAMES TEACHERS PLAY

*Minecraft*,[158] another example of adapting games for education, 'is an open-world game that promotes creativity, collaboration, and problem-solving in an immersive environment'.

> *Minecraft* is a game where you dig (mine) and build (craft) different kinds of 3D blocks within a large world of varying terrains and habitats to explore. In this world the sun rises and sets as you go about your work, gathering materials and making tools. There is rain and the occasional lightning storm, and animals that you can tame, farm, or use for food. Depending on which mode you're playing in, you might also need to fight for your survival against hunger, danger and bad guys.

A typical lesson that educators would use would include clear learning objectives, well-defined tasks and a way to assess progress. An example would be learning economics with *Minecraft*,[159] in which 8-10 year olds would learn to 'define productive resources; give examples of natural, human, and capital resources; apply the use of productive resources as they build a house in *Minecraft* and demonstrate understanding of how uses of productive resources can enhance or diminish end products.' The key skills being developed include 'Critical Thinking, Collaboration and Citizenship.' The example includes detailed resources for students and educators including descriptions, visualizations, assets and assessments. It maps the lesson to defined content standards such as the Common Core standards.

The Institute of Play,[160] New York, is another great example. With the mission of transforming education through play, the Institute has released several games, online and offline (printed board games). In 'The

---

158 Minecraft, Education Edition, retrieved on October 28, 2017 from Microsoft, https://education.minecraft.net/

159 Learning economics with Minecraft, retrieved on October 28, 2017 from https://education.minecraft.net/lessons/learning-economics-minecraft-productive-resources/

160 Institute of Play, retrieved on October 28, 2017 from https://www.instituteofplay.org/

Meaning of Beep,'[161] the gameplay is 'all about the use of context clues to discover the identity of blanked-out words in sentences spoken by a malfunctioning robot named Moby'.

But does playing games, even non-educational ones, mean that skills are being acquired by students? After all, it is not immediately obvious that modes other than poring over textbooks and classroom instruction can have the same effect. The real world transfer of skills from games to learning is well substantiated by learning theorists. Seymour Papert[162] was acknowledged to be 'at the center of three revolutions: child development, artificial intelligence, and computational technologies for education' and is most famously known for his role in development of the programming tool for children called Logo in 1968 and for inspiring brands such as Lego (who made building blocks for children).

Papert was extremely influenced by the work of his mentor, Jean Piaget, who is famously known for his work on Constructivism, the idea that 'children make sense of their world – not as "miniature adults" or empty vessels, but as active agents interacting with the world and building ever-evolving theories'. Papert extended the field of discourse by conceptualizing the theory of Constructionism.

> Constructionism shares constructivism's connotation of learning as 'building knowledge structures' irrespective of the circumstances of the learning. It then adds the idea that this happens especially felicitously in a context where the learner is consciously engaged in constructing a public entity, whether it's a sand castle on the beach or a theory of the universe.

161 The Meaning of Beep, Institute of Play, retrieved on October 28, 2017 from https://www.instituteofplay.org/featured-project-game

162 Groom, Dean (2016), Farewell to the father of computing in colleges, retrieved on April 29, 2019 from https://ccsc.nsw.edu.au/2016/08/04/farewell-father-computing-colleges/. See also Papert, Seymour and Harel, Idit (1991), Chapter 1, Situating Constructionism, Constructionism, Ablex Publishing Corporation, retrieved on April 29, 2019 from http://www.papert.org/articles/SituatingConstructionism.html

Papert believed that learning is doing, rather than just the act of knowing. Rather than 'knowing' it right or wrong, which is what the traditional model of assessment would lead you to believe is the correct way, Papert believed that the way to learn is 'doing' experiments and failing, to practice and reflect on not just the knowledge and skills but how you approach a concept or a problem intellectually and physically.

Michelle Hoyle, a researcher on the *World of Warcraft* especially as it applies to learning, explains how the *World of Warcraft* involves so many different skills that are transferable to real life.[163] She provides a real game scenario where a team of people are going on a quest to destroy two dragons. Team members play different roles - leader of the quest, strategy maker, communications lead and other roles. After every quest, they get together to figure out what they could have done better and they learn to look out for others. They learn to work as a team, leverage collective wisdom and strive to continuously improve their performance. Identity emerges as an important aspect – the true 'real-world' identity of the player, the game identity, and the combination of the two (projected) identities – influence game play and real world transference.

It is not just the students who can benefit from gameplay. The teachers themselves can adopt games and simulations for their own learning. Realistic simulated classroom environments such as the ones developed by Mursion,[164] a company dedicated to building 3D and virtual reality experiences for training and assessment across a wide variety of sectors including education, allow teachers to participate in a live class of virtual students (avatars controlled by human actors) to practice their teaching skills and acquire new ones. Observers or coaches can view the session in real-time or asynchronously, and provide direct feedback. Best practices can be modeled and recorded for later viewing. Assess-

163 Hoyle, Michelle (2012). Persist or Die: learning in World of Warcraft, retrieved on October 28, 2017 from http://einiverse.eingang.org/2012/08/08/persist-or-die/

164 Mursion in Action, Education, retrieved on December 16, 2017 from https://mursion.com/industries/education.html

ments can be created that certify teachers at each level of proficiency and build their expertise in newer models of teaching.

It does seem inappropriate to skew all the innovation in teaching and learning towards students. After all, teachers are also lifelong learners. Their own learning can be augmented immensely by play. Innovative use of all the modern education technologies should equally focus on teachers for their continuous professional development. The same applies to administrators, who can be helped to become better and more effective leaders through play.

Learning with play has tremendous pedagogical value and potential. It can improve learning outcomes and is also an important ingredient for developing 21$^{st}$ century skills. In the hands of skilled educators, it can transform the level of engagement in the classroom and beyond. For this to become a reality at scale, teachers really need to start playing serious games with their students, gamifying their classroom activities and teaching their students real-life skills in safe-to-fail simulated environments.

# #9

# What*If*

## schools made all their labs and experimentation open?

## #9 WHAT*IF* SCHOOLS MADE ALL THEIR LABS AND EXPERIMENTATION OPEN?

*School labs are traditionally closed, insulated environments. Their curriculum is slow to change. Projects are usually premeditated and predictable. Assessments are usually liberal. What if the activities in these labs were to be made open to a wider community? What if experiments and activities outside the curriculum were encouraged widely?*

*What if innovation was shared? What if the world contributed to building tinkering skills and scientific attitudes in each school lab? What if students were able to extend their 'doing' skills beyond the lab? What if the entire world could become a giant lab?*

Imagine you are a scientist working on a new serum to cure a deadly disease. It is part of your daily work in your lab, to research scientific papers in your focus area, conduct experiments and trials and analyze results. You will also typically use software tools to run simulations and conduct data analysis. You will meticulously document your work. You will identify or generate hypotheses and find evidence to support or destroy them. You will analyze claims and counter-claims.

Or, imagine you are a social science researcher who is researching a particular area of ethnographic interest. You would again exhibit many skills such as investigative, analytical, deductive and experimental skills. The world, its resources, its people and your surveys would be your lab just like the equipment and trials would be for the scientist.

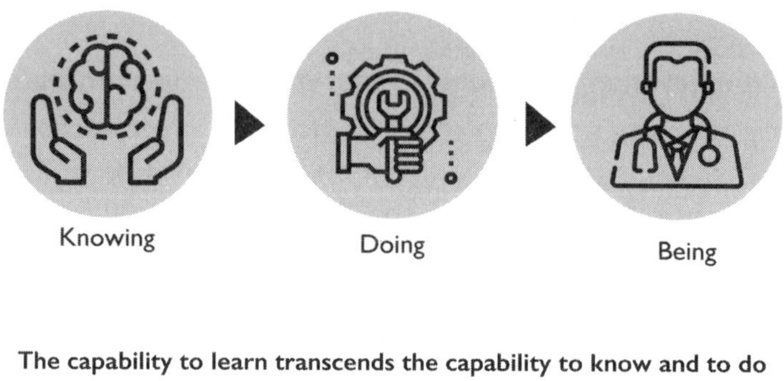


**Figure 17: From Knowing to Being**

Which one of these two images would you find similarity within your school labs? How much of learning to 'be' (say, a scientist or a social science researcher) instead of just learning to 'do' (an experiment prescribed in the curriculum), or learning to 'know' (concepts), is part of your school lab? How much of this would really be openly shared with others? How much of this would be influenced by what others are doing in their labs? How connected are these activities with the real world?

## LABS AND LEARNING

It is a wonder that schools track and publish everything of note but almost never the experimentation of their students and the work they do in their labs, projects, and educational field trips. The higher the students move up the curriculum ladder, the more formal and guided are the experiments and activities they do, but those activities are hidden, unshared, and almost never a part of the students' own portfolio. It is perhaps because schools place an inordinately large focus on learning to know, rather than learning by 'doing' or learning to 'be'.

Experimentation in the classroom, the school lab or in controlled environments such as field trips is extremely important, but usually less rigorously evaluated than the pure scholastic aspect. It is mostly hidden from view unlike the 'lecture' or 'lesson plan' where most of our focus and energies have been concentrated. A key demand of the 21st century is an appreciation, understanding and capability for experimentation, innovation and creation – skills that our social scientists, researchers, scientists, mathematicians and engineers of the future, will initially learn in the lab (or, in general, by 'doing' or 'making'). In fact, aided by continuously evolving and new technologies at scale, the world can be one giant lab.

Less rigor in and for labs is compounded by skill, materials and infrastructure inadequacies. Some of the inadequacies can be explained by lack of funding, some by lack of training and awareness, and some by the fact that our teachers experienced the same deficit when they were students. It can also have some serious consequences. For example, safety in school and college labs is an important consideration the world over – after all many experiments naturally involve some (or a lot of) amount of physical danger and potential harm to our environment. The deficit in labs also translates to poorer learning outcomes, because students cannot relate real world phenomena to what they are learning in class. Lack of attention to learning by doing is also compounded by the nature of assessments in this space, which are manual and largely subjective in nature, and by the slow speed of curricular reform for labs.

There are various definitions of Labs. They could be the formal dedicated spaces in schools equipped with materials and devices where students spend some time each week doing experiments mandated in the syllabus. They could also be segments of demonstrations in the classroom, where the teacher illustrates or verifies a concept learnt in class through them or uses them to provoke learning. They could also include activities that are done in home settings with readily available materials. Often, they are also activities done as part of educational field trips, physical or virtual.

The domains covered by the labs may differ – arts and humanities, culture and performing arts, language, science, computing and mathematics labs – each have different requirements for infrastructure, content, pedagogy and time. The formats may also differ – experiments, projects and other formats may be used in individual or group student formations. The outputs may be thrown away or preserved, and may be formally graded or informally discussed with feedback. They may be a part and parcel of classroom instruction or given dedicated slots in the timetable.

The common underlying principles remain the same. Lab work is an investigation into phenomena surrounding concepts, a verification and reinforcement of things learnt in the classroom, and also a mechanism to explore new phenomena, as yet not encountered by the student. It builds several skills necessary for the 21$^{st}$ Century, whether the student ends up becoming a professional maker (say, a scientist, researcher, inventor or writer) or not. These skills include competencies such as critical thinking, inquiry, problem solving, creativity, teamwork, social awareness, and research.

Labs enhance the capability to understand the nature of the domain and its real-world manifestations. Students learn to frame the research questions, establish the environment for research, make formal observations, conduct physical or thought experimentation to verify hypotheses, capture data, generate insights, and then finally attempt to explain them in terms of the domain knowledge they are acquiring in class. By creating space for labs, educators help students make the real-world connect. They are perhaps as important as the lecture and the test, and are to be seen in an integrated, rather than competing fashion or in any way inferior in terms of the rigor of assessment.

## LABS IN PRACTICE

Let us see what happens in practice. In *America's Lab Report,*[165] created by the National Academy of Sciences in 2006, many important points are made about school science labs. In general, the experts see the classroom and the lab as isolated experiences for the science student (separation between the processes of science and the concepts of science). The research examines instructional design (or how instructional units should be designed and organized) for labs and finds that procedures are emphasized much more than the learning goals, active reflection, and innovation – a kind of 'rote labs' (if you can think of a parallel with rote learning or rote teaching).

The root causes lie in infrastructure and access, training of educators, lack of agreement around the goals and definitions of lab experiences, inimical student-equipment ratios and less time spent in earlier classes on labs than in the later years. Their conclusion is that 'the quality of current laboratory experiences is poor for most students.'

In India, the statistics are dismal. Only 24 percent of schools have both an electricity connection and computing facilities. Nearly 40 percent of 1.4 million schools do not have electricity connections.[166] In a survey[167] of 240,000 schools for classes 11 and 12 (the last two years of

165 Singer, S.R., M.L. Hilton, and H.A. Schweingruber, Eds. (2006). ***America's lab report: Investigations in high school science.*** Washington, DC: The National Academies Press, retrieved on October 29, 2017 from http://nap.edu/11311

166 Flash Statistics 2015-16, NUEPA, retrieved on April 30, 2019 from http://udise.in/Downloads/Publications/Documents/Flash_Statistics-2015-16_(Elementary).pdf

167 Varma, Subodh (2014). 75 percent of schools lack decent science labs: Survey, *The Times of India*, retrieved on October 29, 2017 from https://timesofindia.indiatimes.com/india/75-of-schools-lack-decent-science-labs-Survey/articleshow/40385273.cms?from=mdr

school), it was found that more than 75 percent of schools do not have a fully equipped Science Lab, and for classes nine and 10 this number is quite alarming at over 58 percent. This varies from state to state, with states like Karnataka having just six percent of their schools having fully equipped Labs. Only 7-8 percent of schools have a separate mathematics or language lab. With a more even split of government vs. privately owned schools at higher classes, the responsibility for fixing this is a shared one.

How can we provide access to affordable, high quality labs, expose students to tinkering and experimentation in different and shared ways, and reduce the gap between processes and concepts? How can we accomplish this across subjects, not just for science and mathematics?

Many innovative measures have been employed to address the infrastructure problem. *Vidnyanvahini* (or a 'vehicle for science', literally) has literally employed a mobile strategy for labs through its Mobile Science Lab program addressed at rural secondary science classrooms.[168]

> Typically, members of the Dialogue and Action Group (DAG) of *Vidnyanvahini* together with the local science teachers interact with about eighty students on a given day. The students watch and perform 20 to 25 short experiments. Supplemental information is provided through audio-visual aids, exhibits such as a model electric train, lecture/demonstrations, powerpoint based presentations using laptop/ LCD projector, and classroom discussions.

About 85 schools are covered each year using this methodology and students over grades 8, 9 and 10 (ages 13-15) are covered. Teacher training and online resources also form part of this initiative.

168 Mobile Science Labs, Vidnyanvahini, retrieved on April 30, 2019 from http://www.vidnyanvahini.org/mobile-science-lab.php

Sahayata Trust,[169] supported by Tech Mahindra Foundation in India, also runs an initiative called the Mobile Science Lab, along similar principles as *Vidnyanvahini*. It has over 350 experiments in astronomy, biology, chemistry, physics and mathematics for grades 8-10, aligned to the prominent education board in the country, CBSE. It also has a large number of experiment videos available online. A team of 4-6 postgraduates are accompanied by a professor in each one of their nine visits to 18 schools every year.

A notable, large scale initiative in this space is run by the Agastya Foundation in India. They take 'imaginative and innovative hands-on science education, project-based and peer-to-peer learning to schools, towns and villages across India.'[170] They impact over 10 million children and 250,000 teachers. Agastya has many delivery mechanisms. The Science centers are venues in urban and semi-urban locations where students and teachers can visit to explore various phenomena and engage in hands-on activities. The reach of the mobile labs is immense, '...In a single year, a mobile lab can reach 9,000 to 10,000 children, for a total of more than 20,000 exposures, and 300 exposures for teachers.'

Of particular interest is low cost experimentation. The cost of materials and equipment can become prohibitive, and so can their maintenance and preservation. Agastya and many other such organizations have worked on designing and producing low cost experiments and equipment. The benefits are many – lower costs of materials and equipment, ease of repair and better availability of spares, higher local relevance to curriculum, and flexible adaptation to new concepts. The author was part of one such project at Delhi University in the 1990s called the Locally Produced Low Cost Equipment project, a UNESCO initiative led by Professor Krishna Sane, where equipment such as pH meters,

169 Mobile Science Lab, Sahayata Trust, retrieved on April 30, 2019 from http://mobilesciencelab.in

170 Agastya International Foundation, retrieved on October 29, 2017 from http://www.agastya.org/

conductometers, and calorimeters for chemistry experiments were designed and manufactured locally, and teachers were trained in the assembly, use and maintenance of the kits.

This project also investigated small-scale chemistry kits and green chemistry kits, which have the added advantage of being compact and environmentally safe. In small-scale chemistry kits, chemical reagents are scaled down a thousand times in mass and volume as compared to traditional labs. Glassware use is replaced by reusable plastic or polymers and used to create, for example, microburettes and micropipettes.[171]

Self-contained labs are another interesting innovation. These are Labs that can support whole-class experimentation and may not need external resources such as electricity to run. These Labs contain many varieties of materials and the required apparatus to enable teachers to demonstrate experiments to students across various grades. They are generally portable and easily maintained, and can come with support materials for teachers. There are also fixed options, like a converted teacher's desk cum Lab station. An example is Nano Science Labs[172] from India.

Another wonderful example is in the use of everyday materials for learning science. An initiative called Toys from Trash,[173] by Arvind Gupta in India, investigates how to use materials readily available to explore key concepts in science. Teachers and students could use materials like wood, cycle rims, discarded CDs, nuts and bolts to

171 What is small-scale Chemistry?, retrieved on April 29, 2019 from http://www.smallscalechemistry.colostate.edu/what_is_ssc.html

172 Portable Science Lab in your Classroom, Your story, retrieved on July 15, 2018 from https://yourstory.com/video/portable-science-lab/

173 Toys from Trash, Arvind Gupta Toys, retrieved on October 31, 2017 from http://www.arvindguptatoys.com/toys.html

recreate Foucault's Pendulum,[174] for example, a simple device to show the rotation of the Earth. Similarly, the Hole in the Wall[175] experiment in the 1990s, when Dr. Sugata Mitra decided to place a personal computer in the boundary wall of his office at NIIT in Delhi, India, and leave it to be interpreted and used by the children in the slum next door, provided valuable insights into how students could absorb unfamiliar experiences and make them their own. Another great example is *JodoGyan,*[176] a non-profit initiative run by Shaji and Usha Menon since 1998, which is focused on Mathematics education and has reached over 21,000 schools and 70,000 teachers. They have created teacher education programs, physical kits, and online resources for helping children in school appreciate and enjoy Mathematics.

In the area of computer labs, there has been a natural evolution in two directions. First, the last few years have seen the emergence of many new programming languages and architectures. There is a paradigm shift towards cloud computing and full stack programming using languages such as Go, Python and Node.js. This has given rise to online coding simulators (where students can learn and practice coding) and to events around coding (such as hackathons – a marathon session where coders are invited to build their response to a challenge thrown at them; also now a popular mechanism for recruitment). There has been large scale participation on online MOOC (massive open online courses) platforms such as *Coursera* and *edX*. India is the largest source of this demand outside the USA and the bulk of the demand is for technical courses. Students and professionals have jumped at the idea of learning technology online. However most computer curricula, and the associated textbooks, have largely ignored these developments, or still continue to use old content.

174 Foucault's Pendulum, Toys from Trash, retrieved on October 31, 2017 from http://www.arvindguptatoys.com/toys/Pendulum.html

175 The Guardian (2016, June 7). Sugata Mitra – The professor with his head in the cloud, *The Guardian*, 2016, retrieved on April 30, 2019 from https://www.theguardian.com/education/2016/jun/07/sugata-mitra-professor-school-in-cloud

176 Jodogyan, retrieved on October 29, 2017 from http://jodogyan.org/

Second, the concept of what goes into the IT lab is undergoing a slow change – from just rows of desktop computers connected with each other in a local network with intermittent connectivity to the Internet to always connected systems, new types of devices such as 3D printers, mobile devices, and sensors, backed by access to a variety of cloud computing resources. It is a slow but sure change in the landscape that is opening up new knowledge and creation possibilities.

There have been a variety of solutions for labs – from individual home use 'kit' formats to whole-class and Lab formats, supported by digital options, spanning various age levels. Over the past few years the digital 'makerspaces' have also gained a formidable reputation. Sites such as *Instructables*[177] collect do-it-yourself activities across a wide range of activities and engage an entire community of enthusiasts. Topics could range from technology to cooking and the arts and contributors regardless of age, are joined together by the desire to share and learn from other makers. Contributors are able to provide step-by-step construction instructions along with images and videos and the community is able to comment and rate these contributions. These 'makerspaces' liberate the experiment from the confined space of the school or the garage, and make them open and available for the entire world to learn from and improve.

As a direct corollary, '*makerspaces*' also lend themselves to ideas for incubation and professional development and a way to gain repute for expert contributors. Many new 'kit' based solutions have also emerged that encourage learning by doing. Even the more ubiquitous robotic programming solutions are transforming with the help of more connected and intelligent devices, software and components.

177 Instructables, retrieved on October 29, 2017 from http://www.instructables.com/

## STEM AND EXPERIENTIAL LEARNING

STEM (Science, Technology, Engineering and Mathematics) learning and teaching – an integrated view of these disciplines – is gaining rapid acceptance among educators. STEM educators realize that making students visualize the links between these disciplines and to the careers they could choose when they graduate, is really important. Worldwide, there is a shortage of STEM graduates and this directly impacts the progress of entire nations.

The World Is Running Out Of Steam
21st Century Skills. Makerspaces. Integrated Curricula.

**Figure 18: STEAM is steadily gaining national level importance**

In the UK, less than 17 percent of the students in the 10-14 age group aspire for a career in STEM and the proportion of A-level pupils studying STEM have remained lower than what the number was ten years ago.[178]

178 Improving young people's engagement with science, technology, engineering and mathematics (STEM), NFER Thinks, What the Evidence tells us, 2013, retrieved on October 29, 2017 from https://www.stem.org.uk/system/files/elibrary-resources/legacy_files_migrated/26969-Improving%20young%20peoples%20engagement%20with%20stem.pdf

Around 20 percent of the UK workforce is employed in STEM-related occupations - about 5.8 million people (about 4.3 million in engineering alone). Out of 650,000 students taking the GCSE in the UK, only about 7,000 professional engineers are produced.[179] It is projected that work, in the future, will require more STEM knowledge and skills such as critical thinking, logic and mathematical reasoning than ever before, and that demand is already outstripping the supply.

In the USA, estimates suggest that at least 20 percent of the workforce is in STEM-related careers. Employment in these occupations is projected to grow to more than nine million between 2012 and 2022. At about 13 percent growth, STEM jobs are predicted to be the fastest growing segment.[180] According to a White House report,[181] 'studies show that less than half of schools offered computer programming, and nearly 40 percent of high schools did not offer physics in 2015. Additionally, STEM and Computer Science education among women, minorities, and students in rural communities are limited.'

The focus on STEM is echoed by many countries including India and China, both nations aspiring to be world leaders in science and technology by leveraging the large numbers of students in their education systems. According to the India Science Report,[182] only 13.4 percent of students in class 11 and 12 (ages 16-18) said they would like to take up pure science in later years as opposed to 22 percent of students in

179 The UK STEM education landscape, Royal Academy of Engineers (2016), retrieved on October 29, 2017 from http://www.raeng.org.uk/publications/reports/uk-stem-education-landscape

180 Viloria, Dennis (2014, Spring). STEM 101: Intro to tomorrow's jobs, *Occupational Outlook Quarterly*, retrieved on April 29, 2019 from http://www.stemedcoalition.org/wp-content/uploads/2010/05/BLS-STEM-Jobs-report-spring-2014.pdf

181 President Trump signs memorandum for STEM education funding, 26 September 2017, retrieved on October 31, 2017 from https://www.whitehouse.gov/blog/2017/09/26/president-trump-signs-memorandum-stem-education-funding

182 Shukla, Rajesh (2005). India science report, science education, human resources and public attitude towards science and technology, National Council of Applied Economic Research, 2005, retrieved on April 30, 2019 from http://www.insaindia.res.in/pdf/India_Science_report-Main.pdf

class 6-8. Student interest in the sciences is low and 40 percent of class 11-12 students are not satisfied with the quality of science teaching. In Computer Science, the satisfaction ratio falls even lower with only 15-23 percent students being satisfied with the quality of teaching. The situation may not have changed much in the past decade. No Indian scholar working in an Indian university has received a Nobel Prize since 1930, when C V Raman got it.[183]

Initiatives such as the Hoshangabad Science Teaching Programme (HSTP), which covered over 1,000 schools across 16 districts in India before it was unceremoniously shut down,[184] have shaped the discourse on science education in the country.

> An important difference between the HSTP and conventional science teaching is that the former emphasized the processes of science — observation, recording, performing controlled experiments, etc. On the other hand, conventional school science emphasizes the "products" of science — laws, theories, etc. In some sense the process-product debate continues to this day, with the mainstream in favor of teaching products.

Teacher education is viewed as a critical factor in STEM education.[185] One of the problems in India has been the isolation of teacher preparation from formal universities. It is considered more as a professional stream than as a symbiotic part of a microcosm of research and innovation that is the university. Increased privatization and the gap between pedagogy and subject matter expertise are other important causes of problems with science teaching.

---

183 Science education in India, D R Bhagat, quoting the then Indian President Pranab Mukherjee, 07 March 2017, retrieved on October 31, 2017 from http://www.dailyexcelsior.com/science-education-india/

184 Mukherjee, Amitabha (2007). Science education in India, *The Hindu*, 16 August 2007, retrieved on October 31, 2017 from http://www.thehindu.com/todays-paper/tp-opinion/Science-education-in-India/article14816775.ece

185 Subramaniam, K (2016). Institutions of higher education and research in India: Do they need to take interest in school science education?, *Current Science*, 111(10), 1575–1576, retrieved on October 31, 2017 from http://www.currentscience.ac.in/Volumes/111/10/1575.pdf

Initiatives that strengthen infrastructure and access, that develop a healthy teacher education system, that focus equally on both processes and products of science (and other domains in STEM) and that are more aligned to 21$^{st}$ century skills and the future of work, are the need of the hour, worldwide. This is why many governments have rapidly started investing in STEM education and teacher professional development.

As a case in point, the Indian government has started the Atal Tinkering Labs (ATL).[186] Under the ATL scheme, each approved school gets a grant of about USD 30,000 over five years, half the amount going in the establishment of a formal lab space with equipment including Arduino microprocessors, sensors and a wide variety of tools, and the other half to conducting events and promoting a maker culture through events and maker fairs. About 2,500 schools have been targeted across government and private schools. The vision is to cultivate one million children in India as neoteric inventors.

In the USA, as another example, President Obama called on the nation to 'develop, recruit, and retain 100,000 excellent STEM teachers over the next 10 years' and 'also has asked colleges and universities to graduate an additional one million students with STEM majors'. The STEM 2026 vision report by the US Department of Education proposes some measures for improving STEM education such as innovative measures of learning, flexible learning spaces, solving relevant grand challenges, promoting diversity, accessible activities that invite play and risk, and engaged and networked communities of practice.[187] In September 2017, President Trump signed a memorandum[188] for STEM education, with

---

186 Niti Aayog (2017). Atal Tinkering Labs, retrieved on October 31, 2017 from http://niti.gov.in/content/atal-tinkering-laboratories

187 STEM 2026, A vision for innovation in STEM Education, Department of Education, USA, 2015, retrieved on October 29, 2017 from https://innovation.ed.gov/files/2016/09/AIR-STEM2026_Report_2016.pdf

188 Presidential Memorandum for the Secretary of Education, September 25, 2017, retrieved on October 31, 2017 from https://www.whitehouse.gov/the-press-office/2017/09/25/memorandum-secretary-education

committed funding to the tune of USD 200 million annually and with a special focus on computer science teaching.

With such a focus on STEM that is emerging worldwide, it is logical to consider the ingredients for success of STEM programs, particularly in their design and in their capability to scale.

**Figure 19: STEAM pedagogies can leverage new age technology**

One interesting use of new distributed technologies is the Internet of Things (IoT) – the billions of devices ('things') that are connected together on the Internet. These could include specialized devices like weather stations, or could be everyday appliances such as the mobile phone, refrigerator, or car. If they are connected via the Internet, they become a source of specific information that can be used for educational (and other) purposes. They can also be remotely controlled and configured, which makes them easily adaptable to various needs.

A great example of educational use is The Internet of School Things,[189] a website that provides access to IoT devices that could be situated anywhere, and to generate relevant data for experiments. In one experiment that investigated prolonged drought conditions leading to

189 The Internet of School Things, retrieved on October 31, 2017 from http://iotschool.org/experiment.php?id=KuFqe

water shortages, a group of people collected data polled via these IoT devices to predict the onset of the monsoon. As another example, the HiTemp project of the Birmingham Urban Climate Lab at the University of Birmingham,[190] uses a vast network of sensors to study Birmingham's Urban Heat Island.

This is reminiscent of the series of stories on the use of the Internet for education, by WestEd in 1996, called the 'Tales from the Electronic Frontier.'[191] In one of the stories, they provided a case study of two groups of school students located at different places that came together virtually to experimentally determine the shape of the Earth. Like Eratosthenes did many hundreds of years ago (200 BCE), they decided they will measure the shadows that objects cast at different points of the day. They then collated their findings, and made the mathematical jump required to determine the curvature of the Earth between their two school locations.

The IoT world is enhanced by the use of wearables – technologies such as rings, smart watches and bands that are worn on the body and can report data on position, speed and health.[192] Technologies like Google Glass are examples of experience captures and can be used for learning expeditions or for recording experiences on the go.[193] Augmented reality could help provide feedback to students to tell them if they are doing the right thing when constructing a real world object or conducting an experiment. They can, even, in more intrusive settings, utilize body-kinesthetic indicators to give tactile feedback. More administrative side use cases can include attendance and tracking.

---

190 Birmingham Urban Climate Lab, retrieved on April 30, 2019 from https://www.birmingham.ac.uk/schools/gees/centres/bucl/index.aspx

191 Tall Shadows, Tales from the Electronic Frontier, WestEd, retrieved on October 31, 2017 from http://files.eric.ed.gov/fulltext/ED400776.pdf

192 Elton, Keith (2017). Wearable tech in the classroom: Taking the education industry by storm, *eLearning Industry*, April 9, 2017, retrieved on October 31, 2017 from https://elearningindustry.com/wearable-tech-in-the-classroom-taking-education-industry-storm

193 TeachThought Staff (2015, December 28). 36 ways to use wearable technology in the classroom, *TeachThought,* retrieved on October 31, 20017 from https://www.teachthought.com/technology/36-ways-to-use-wearable-technology-in-the-classroom/

Another great example of the real-world connect using technology is in real-life expeditions, modeled through technology-enabled real world experiences or through virtual reality and augmented reality models. Polar Husky[194] is an example of the former. This is an annual series of Arctic expeditions in which a team of researchers lead educational expeditions that are streamed live to classrooms. Students can view the progress of the expedition and explore local culture, flora and fauna, weather and a host of real-world phenomena. Students learn geography, mathematics, arts, English, and science in an inter-disciplinary and real-life manner. More importantly, they begin to appreciate the life of a researcher and what it means to be like one.

Such experiences allow individual education explorers to create fascinating real-life experiences for students anywhere in the world. For areas hard to access or situations hard to recreate, there is the world of virtual reality, where sophisticated 3D models and wearable VR technology is used to recreate (say) an extinct phenomenon such as the Harappa civilization.

Then there is 3D printing – the ability to design and construct (print) 3D models. 3D printing has given rise to great learning and making opportunities in the classroom.[195] Using 3D printers, students could, for example, construct a model of the layers of the earth[196] (inner core, outer core, mantle, and crust) and physically print its 3D model to use in class. They could also share the same design so that other students across the world could use and extend it. 3D printing also enables students to express their creativity and ingenuity, by allowing them to create models of things that work according to accepted scientific and aesthetic principles, but which may have no existing equivalent in the real world.

---

194 Free Adventure learning for the classroom, retrieved on April 30, 2019 from http://2011.polarhusky.com/

195 Adams, Jessica (2016). 7 Fun and easy lesson plans to jumpstart 3D printing in your classroom, retrieved on October 31, 2017 from https://www.makerbot.com/media-center/2016/06/03/lesson-plans-steam-learning

196 Cutaway earth model, February 21, 2004, retrieved on October 31, 2017 from https://www.thingiverse.com/thing:254628

*Drones in education*[197] is another idea that is extremely powerful to explore. By their very nature, drones can be carriers of sensing devices, can capture images and video through aerial photography, be used to demonstrate scientific concepts such as speed and momentum, and 'drones can be used to help enhance orientation skills, motor skills, and even give students a better understanding of how the world around us works.'[198]

> In Haridas Chandran's (who is a physical science teacher at Belfry school in West Virginia, USA) aerospace class, for example, students learned to build wind tunnels out of wooden planks and then used them to test how air currents support flying machines. The kids cemented their newfound aviation knowledge with a trip to a local airport to see airplanes in action. Not surprisingly, Chandran's students also mastered the science of building and flying drones.

Projects like these, involve the study of real-world phenomena (could be virtual too) using the Internet of Things or other technology affordances, and bind the processes of science into the products of science being taught in the classroom. They build not just the technical knowledge, but also the skills to collaborate in a digital network, across cultures. They build vital 21st century skills and the capability to capture, interpret and analyze data – a critical competence today. When performed in a manner that is open and shared, this approach has the potential to scale STEM education to very large and diverse audiences. Combined with 'making' which gives the capability to anyone to author and contribute to activities, it becomes a powerful tool in the design of STEM education.

Makerspaces, when harnessed to solve real-world problems, become even more meaningful for students. At the Learning Paths School in

---

197 Wolpert-Gawron, Heather (2005, November12). Drones can be fun – and educational, *Edutopia,* retrieved on April 30, 2019 from https://www.edutopia.org/blog/7-ways-use-drones-classroom-heather-wolpert-gawron

198 Nix, Naomi (2017, August 18). The value of bringing drones to the classroom, *The Atlantic*, retrieved on April 30, 2019 from https://www.theatlantic.com/education/archive/2017/08/the-value-of-bringing-drones-to-the-classroom/537150/

India, ably led by Robin Aggarwal, students have created models that can be used to demonstrate educational concepts in low-cost classrooms in rural India, a wonderful way to use makerspaces to create solutions for education itself.

By making creating, tinkering, and exploration a shared and open endeavor, schools can make labs truly open. It is, perhaps, time to make the world one giant LAB!

# #10

# What*If*

## MOOCs actually worked?

# #10 WHAT*IF* MOOCS ACTUALLY WORKED?

*Massive Open Online Courses or MOOCs have rapidly gained both worldwide fame and notoriety. Fame because the pundits promised a brave new world of free online quality education for all. Notoriety because they have as yet not lived up to their promise. What are the reasons for this?*

*Did the more popular and more recent forms of the MOOC really follow the beliefs, practices, and conviction of its founders? What if they had really been inspired by them? What if they had believed in a better educational future instead of being hungry for Internet scale success? What if their models and motivation had truly followed the founders as they attempted to research and build an alternative education future?*

**It's 2011**. The great rebranding of online higher education has already started. Massive Open Online Course (MOOC) providers are the new blue-eyed girls and boys of the Internet era. Will this be the revolution everyone has been waiting for?

Just two years later, a great furore has erupted around MOOCs. Nearly everyone is citing high dropout rates as their single largest failure. There is an academic backlash about their effectiveness and they are no longer believed to be a serious alternative to the traditional educational system.

Perhaps, the critics may have been looking at MOOCs from a different lens than they should have used. They may have been ignoring the hordes that had dropped 'in' just to sample a new educational experience – quite an achievement in itself even in the non-formal world, at scale and online.

## THE POPULAR HISTORY OF MOOCS

But what are MOOCs and why are they called so? MOOCs are online courses offered by some of the best universities and professionals across the world. They are massive, in the sense that they are subscribed to by large numbers of people. They are open, in the sense that anyone can join a course from anywhere in the world without restrictions. They are online, so if you have an Internet connection and a device to play the course content, you can access them. They are also structured as regular online courses and may even include academic support from teaching assistants and teachers/experts online. They allow collaboration in the form of discussion forums and social feeds. At the end of the course, you could decide to get formal certification by appearing for an exam, which would either be entirely online, or facilitated offline in a testing center. The certificate would be given by the originating university, the instructor who created the course, or by the MOOC platform itself. It is likely that you would pay for the certification, but not the course itself, which would be free.

This is an innovation over other forms of online and distance learning courses which have pay-walls around content and require subscriptions or purchase to access. It is also an innovation over open education resources (OER) like the MIT Open Courseware,[199] in the sense that it provides a course-led experience rather than a bank of content resources.

Sebastian Thrun, Director of the Stanford Artificial Intelligence Laboratory till 2011 and later head of Google X, an ambitious Google project, created *KnowLabs*, considered the first company to get into MOOCs. Thrun realized that out of the nine elements of a course (admissions, lectures, peer interaction, professor interaction, problem-solving, assignments, exams, deadlines, and certification), MIT Open Courseware handled only one element well – the recorded classroom lectures[200] (and/or notes) along with some additional resources. That is, the course materials, in some forms, were placed in OER repositories for access and reference by anyone, but they were not a course you could take in the sense of a traditional course, with start and end times, periodic assessments and instructor support. In India, a similar case exists with the National Program on Technology Enhanced Learning (NPTEL)[201] which followed a similar approach.

Thrun was probably inspired by the discovery of Khan Academy and its promotion by Bill Gates. He teamed up with his colleague Peter Norvig, Google's Director of Research and his co-professor in the graduate level course from Stanford, CS221: Introduction to Artificial Intelligence. In June, 2011 he founded *KnowLabs*, and soon the online course version was available for students from anywhere in the world. The response far exceeded any initial estimates that Thrun and Norvig had made.

---

199 MIT Open Courseware, retrieved on November 12, 2017 from https://ocw.mit.edu/index.htm

200 Leckart, Steven (2012, February 3). The Stanford education experiment could change higher learning forever, *Science*, retrieved on November 12, 2017 from https://www.wired.com/2012/03/ff_aiclass/all/

201 NPTEL, retrieved on November 12, 2017 from http://nptel.ac.in/

By the middle of August, 2011, enrolment had crossed 100,000 students, an exponential jump over the few hundreds of students they had taught in classrooms over the years. Figuring that this could probably also become a sustainable business opportunity, Thrun started investigating revenues from sources other than students paying for the materials and access – such as placement programs. The basic premise was to keep the courseware free, but perhaps charge for services such as coaching, placement, and certification. *KnowLabs* raised money in December 2011 and built a platform they called *Udacity*, a combination of 'audacious' and 'university', believing that this idea would revolutionize higher education worldwide.

Meanwhile, two other professors from Stanford - Daphne Koller and Andrew Ng - had similar ideas. In April 2012, *Coursera*[202] was launched, inspired by the popular class Ng taught on Machine Learning, just like Thrun's Artificial Intelligence class. The first edition of this course online attracted over 100,000 students and continues to be a very popular course even today with over two million students enrolled since 2011. The difference in approach from *Udacity* was that *Coursera* was focused on building university partnerships from the very beginning. Its goal was to partner with the top 200 universities in the world and bring their content to everyone for free. By July 2012, *Coursera* had signed up 12 reputed universities in the US and Europe.[203] Like *Udacity*, *Coursera* attracted very early interest from investors and raised a lot of capital.

---

202 Gannes, Liz (2012, April 18). Stanford professors launch Coursera with $16M From Kleiner Perkins and NEA, *AllThingsD*, retrieved on November 12, 2017 from http://allthingsd.com/20120418/stanford-professors-launch-coursera-with-16m-from-kleiner-perkins-and-nea/

203 Jeevan Vasagar (2012, July 17). Top universities join free online teaching platform, *The Guardian*, retrieved on April 30, 2019 from https://www.theguardian.com/education/2012/jul/17/top-universities-free-online-classes

Not wanting to be left out, MIT and Harvard quickly followed suit with the May 2012 launch of *edX*,[204] a non-profit initiative by both universities to bring their courses online for free. *edX* was based on *MITx*, an initiative announced in December 2011.[205] *edX* built its own model for sustainability by partnering with universities worldwide (including India's prestigious Indian Institute of Technology, Bombay).

Close on their heels, the Open University, UK, with a long tradition of OER and distance learning, joined the bandwagon by launching *FutureLearn*[206] in December 2012 with the participation of 21 UK universities. France followed in October, 2013[207] with an announcement that it would use the Open *edX* platform (the open source version of *edX*) to create its national MOOCs platform, France Université Numerique. In China, the Tsinghua University-backed *XuetangX*,[208] launched in October 2013,[209] now has over 300 Chinese-language courses. Australia launched *Open2Study* in March 2013, while Italy launched a national platform called *EduOpen*[210] in November 2014. *Edraak*,[211] the Arab MOOC platform, was established in July,

---

204 Gannes, Liz (2012, May 2). Harvard and MIT launch $60m nonprofit online EdX platform, *AllthingsD*, retrieved on April 30, 2019 from http://allthingsd.com/20120502/harvard-and-mit-launch-60m-non-profit-online-edx-platform/

205 MIT News (2011, December 19). MIT launches online learning initiative, *MIT News*, retrieved on November 12, 2017 from http://news.mit.edu/2011/mitx-education-initiative-1219

206 Shaw, Claire (2013, September 18). FutureLearn courses mark UK's entry into global online learning race, *The Guardian*, retrieved on November 12, 2017 from https://www.theguardian.com/higher-education-network/2013/sep/18/futurelearn-open-university-courses-launch

207 edX Press, retrieved on November 12, 2017 from https://www.edx.org/press/edx-work-french-ministry-higher

208 XuetangX, retrieved on November 13, 2017 from http://www.xuetangx.com/global

209 Class Central (2016). XuetangX: A Look at China's First and Biggest MOOC Platform, *Class Central*, October 16, 2016, retrieved on November 13, 2017 from https://www.class-central.com/report/xuetangx/

210 EduOpen, retrieved on April 30, 2019 from https://learn.eduopen.org/?lang=en

211 Edraak, retrieved on November 12, 2017 from https://www.edraak.org/en/about-us/, https://blog.edx.org/queen-rania-foundation-launches-edraak

2014,[212] again in partnership with *edX* as an initiative of the Queen Rania Foundation. *MiríadaX*,[213] a Latin American platform that offers 350 courses in Spanish, was formally launched in July 2014. India launched its national MOOCs platform *SWAYAM* in 2017, bringing together the OER initiatives in the country established under the National Mission on Education through ICT. The *SWAYAM* platform will host up to '2,000 courses and 80,000 hours of learning, covering school, under-graduate, post-graduate, engineering, law and other professional courses.'[214] In 2018, the Israeli Ministry of Social Equality started a MOOC platform called Campus.il[215], based on edX, which has courses in only Hebrew and Arabic. Regional MOOC players are increasing in prominence.

**Figure 20: The buzz surrounding MOOCs**

---

212 edX Press, retrieved on November 12, 2017 from https://www.edx.org/press/saudi-arabia-edx-join-forces-bridge-gap

213 MiriadaX, retrieved on November 12, 2017 from https://miriadax.net/cursos

214 SWAYAM, About, retrieved on November 12, 2017 from https://swayam.gov.in/About

215 Pickard, Laurie (2018). Israeli Government To Launch MOOC Platform for Speakers of Hebrew and Arabic, retrieved on August 12, 2018 from https://www.class-central.com/report/campus-il-mooc-platform/; see https://campus.gov.il/

The MOOCs, backed by venture capital, leading universities and influential persons, succeeded in raising a lot of hype. They were touted to be the next big thing in education, with the potential to revolutionize it. By making the 'best' content and teachers across the world available at no charge, MOOC-makers thought they would shake up the system of education itself. Large investments by private capital and university foundations shaped popular perception about the revolutionary potential of these MOOCs. Also universities viewed them as extending their reach and brand. Open courseware had existed for a very long time, but the shape and form of MOOCs was far more accessible and exciting, and soon became the buzzword.

> Higher education is now being disrupted; our MP3 is the massive open online course (or MOOC), and our Napster is *Udacity*, the education startup.[216] [Clay Shirky]

> Former U.S. Secretary of Education William Bennett has written that he senses 'an Athens-like renaissance' in the making. Stanford president John Hennessy told the New Yorker he sees a 'tsunami coming.'[217] [Nicholas Carr]

> In 50 years, he [Sebastian Thrun] says, there will be only 10 institutions in the world delivering higher education and *Udacity* has a shot at being one of them.[218] [Leckart]

Interestingly *Udacity* pivoted to a new model in 2013.[219] Its high profile experiment with San Jose State University (SJSU) had floundered. In

---

216 Shirky Clay (2012). Napster, Udacity and the Academy, retrieved on November 12, 2017 from http://www.shirky.com/weblog/2012/11/napster-udacity-and-the-academy/

217 Carr, Nicholas (2012, September 27). The crisis in higher education, *MIT Technology Review*, retrieved on November 12, 2017 from https://www.technologyreview.com/s/429376/the-crisis-in-higher-education/

218 Leckart, Steven (2012, February 3). The Stanford education experiment could change higher learning forever, *Science*, retrieved on November 12, 2017 from https://www.wired.com/2012/03/ff_aiclass/all/

219 Watters, Audrey (2013, November 14). Why we shouldn't celebrate Udacity's "Pivot", *Hack Education*, retrieved on November 12, 2017 from http://hackeducation.com/2013/11/14/thrun-as-saint

January 2013, SJSU and *Udacity* had announced a deal in which they would launch a pilot program called San Jose State Plus with three online courses - pre-algebra, college algebra, and elementary statistics. The Bill and Melinda Gates Foundation provided a grant for the pilot. The university would provide academic credits if a student passed. The professors at San Jose State would teach the courses, while *Udacity* would provide the supporting technology, resources, and assistants who would support students. The courses would cost students $150 as opposed to nearly $430 for a regular student.[220] The results were disappointing as they found students performed better in regular classroom courses as opposed to the online cohort of about 300 students – 74 percent students passed in the regular mode compared to only 51 percent enrolled online.[221] The promise of low-cost online and for-credit courses was belied. San Jose State University faculty was critical of the move. Preston Rudy, Vice President of the San Jose State chapter of the California Faculty Association, said the university must be cautious with what he called its experiments on students. 'It's wise to reevaluate and pursue something based on the evidence rather than the advertisement,' he said.[222]

The results could have been so adverse for a number of reasons. One reason could be the composition of the online cohort that included at-risk students, high school students, and SJSU students who had already failed at a remedial math program. The other could have been the haste with which the courses were put together, which led to reduced faculty involvement with the actual course progress because more time had to be spent in creating the materials. But greater scrutiny of these reasons is required. After all a MOOC is all about 'massive' and if we can't

220 Fain, Paul (2013, January 16). As California Goes?, ***Inside Higher Ed***, retrieved on November 12, 2017 from https://www.insidehighered.com/news/2013/01/16/california-looks-moocs-online-push

221 Rivard, Ry (2013, July 18). Udacity project on 'pause', ***Inside HigherEd***, retrieved on November 12, 2017 from https://www.insidehighered.com/news/2013/07/18/citing-disappointing-student-outcomes-san-jose-state-pauses-work-udacity

222 Ibid

prove the pedagogy works at a small scale with this level of diversity in students, or the problems in academic support that may arise at even such a small scale, then something else is probably wrong.

Thrun admitted that they had made a 'lousy product' and made the pivot from formal education to job-training. His claim that only 10 universities or institutions will deliver higher education in 50 years seems to have been erased.[223] Siemens[224] stated that 'No one did more of a disservice to MOOCs than Thrun through his wild proclamations' and:

> Amazingly, after Udacity and Thrun's "bull in a China shop" run through higher education, he proclaims that he has seen the light: "We were on the front pages of newspapers and magazines, and at the same time, I was realizing, we don't educate people as others wished, or as I wished. We have a lousy product…It was a painful moment."
>
> ….He promised us a bright future of open learning. He delivered to us something along the lines of a 1990's corporate elearning program.

In contrast, at SJSU, when *edX* was used to supplement the existing college course (like the open courseware approach), that seemed to work much better. Students using *edX* material with their existing course, performed better than those who did not, although it is not obvious that *edX* is the reason for the better performance.

In India, IIT Bombay professor, Deepak Phatak, figured that the only way to make MOOCs work was to blend them, particularly for engineering education.[225] He was not convinced that the purely online MOOC

---

223 Watters, Audrey (2013, October 15). A future with only 10 universities (Minding the Future, #OpenVA), Hack Education, retrieved on November 12, 2017 from http://hackeducation.com/2013/10/15/minding-the-future-openva

224 Siemens, George (2013, November 15). The failure of Udacity, *eLearnspace*, retrieved on November 12, 2017 from http://www.elearnspace.org/blog/2013/11/15/the-failure-of-udacity/

225 Adopting MOOCs for quality engineering education in India , Dr. Deepak B. Phatak, IIT Bombay, ICTIEE 2014, retrieved on November 12, 2017 from http://www.it.iitb.ac.in/frg/wiki/images/4/48/ICTIEE_Invited_keyynote_BlendedMOOCs_dbphatak_17January2014.pdf

format was working. There were low completion rates, the removal of the formal links with the teacher and the university was dangerous, and the absence of practical (laboratory) sessions was a severe limiting factor. So he proposed a flipped classroom model in which students would engage with content from reputed professors online and teachers would come into class to clear student doubts, provide personalized remediation, organize lab work and mentor projects. Subsequently, both the agencies responsible for university and technical education in India, decided to offer up to 20 percent of credits in any semester of term, through *SWAYAM*.[226] In 2017, the Indian government also announced teacher professional development courses on this platform.

Over the years, *Coursera* and *Udacity*, amongst others, have figured that industry acknowledgement and the support of the MOOCs they offer hold greater potential for monetization. If they can prepare students for jobs and if that preparation is in partnership with industry, students performing well on these courses can fare better in their placement programs. As a result *Udacity* has complete certification paths called *Nano-degrees* (in 2017 they had 50,000 enrolments and 27,000 graduates),[227] *Coursera* has paths called *Specializations*, *edX* has credentials called *MicroMasters* and *FutureLearn* has *Programs*. Needless to state, these are paid certifications. Companies like IBM, Microsoft, and CISCO have been running these certifications for as long as we can remember, albeit behind paywalls.

Another emerging model is that of paid online degrees being offered by universities through platforms such as Coursera and edX. In 2018, the number of online degree based MOOCs went up to 45 (up from 15 in 2017)[228].

---

226 Press Information Bureau, Government of India (2006, December 15), retrieved on April 30, 2019 from http://pib.nic.in/newsite/PrintRelease.aspx?relid=155451

227 Shah, Dhawal (2018, February 28). Udacity's revenues reach $70 million in 2017, *Class Central*, retrieved on April 13, 2018 from https://www.class-central.com/report/udacity-revenues-2017/

228 Shah, Dhawal (2019, January 2), Year of MOOC-based Degrees: A Review of MOOC Stats and Trends in 2018, retrieved on January 06, 2019 from https://www.edsurge.com/amp/news/2019-01-02-year-of-mooc-based-degrees-a-review-of-mooc-stats-and-trends-in-2018. See also, list of online degree based MOOCs at https://www.class-central.com/pricing-charts/mooc-based-degrees

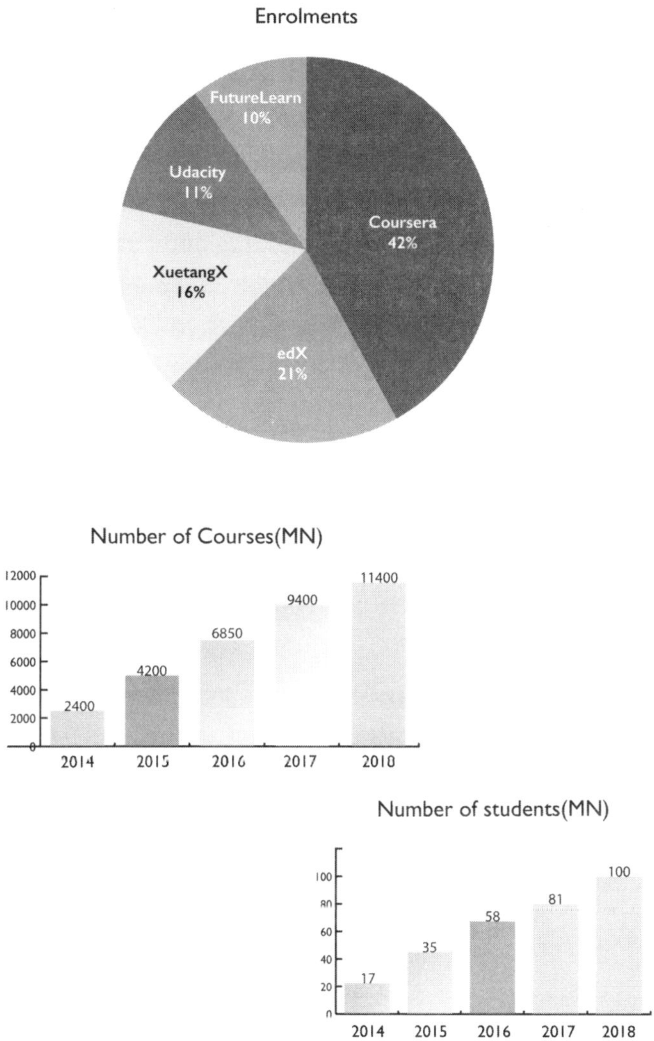


**Figure 21: MOOCs – the evidence through the years 2014-18**

The model that seems to be working is to offer university-supplied credentials (complete degree as well as course credits) at lower costs, with lower entry barriers and more flexibility than on-campus based programs. Despite a lower number of students signing up for MOOCs in 2018 (about 20 mn, down from 23 mn the year before), the number of paying students for these online degrees seem to be on the rise. In 2018, there were over 10,000 students enrolled in MOOC-based degree programs.

In parallel, the focus on corporate training through MOOCs, is also being actively pursued by MOOC providers. Micro-credentials, which lie somewhere between a certificate course and a complete degree program, have been popular with both job aspirants and employees seeking to advance their careers. Over 630 micro-credentials are now in existence, the large majority of them from edX and Coursera.

According to Class Central,[229] a leading MOOC research company, MOOC providers serviced over 100 million students worldwide in 2018, up from 81 million students in 2017, 58 million students in 2016, 35 million students in 2015, and 17 million students in 2014.[230] In 2016, 2,600 new courses (as compared to 1,800 in 2015) were launched, taking the total to about 7,000 online courses offered by over 700 universities worldwide. The total number of courses went up from 2400 in 2014, to 4200 in 2015, 6850 in 2016, 9400 in 2017 and 11400 in 2018. The number of universities participating MOOCs went up from 400+ in 2014, to 500+ in 2015, 700+ in 2016, 800+ in 2017 and 900+ in 2018. Investments in MOOC providers totaled to about USD 400 million by 2016 , and by 2018 just the total of investments in four providers - Coursera, Udacity, Udemy and XeutangX - crossed USD 550 mn. Together, *Coursera*, *Udacity* and *edX* reportedly generated about USD 100 million in revenues in 2016 , while in 2018, Class Central estimated just Coursera's revenue to be USD 140 mn. *Coursera* runs ahead of the pack with 37 million learners and over 3,000 courses, close to the size of the entire Indian higher education enrolment. *edX* is the next largest (18

229 Shah, Dhawal (2018, January 18). By the numbers: MOOCs in 2017, Class-central, retrieved on July 17, 2018 from https://www.class-central.com/report/mooc-stats-2017/. See also reports across years https://www.class-central.com/moocs-year-in-review-2014 (2014),https://www.class-central.com/report/moocs-2015-stats/ (2015), https://www.class-central.com/report/mooc-stats-2016/ (2016) and company websites

230 ICEF Monitor (2017, January 16). Global MOOC Enrolment jumped again last year, *ICEF Monitor*, retrieved on November 12, 2017 from http://monitor.icef.com/2017/01/global-mooc-enrolment-jumped-last-year/

million learners and over 2,100 courses), followed by the Chinese *XuetangX* (14 million learners, 500+ partners and 1,500 courses[231]), *FutureLearn* (8.7 million learners and 480 courses) and *Udacity* (10 million learners). It is interesting to note that India is the largest country outside the US in terms of enrolments for providers such as *edX, Udacity* and *Coursera.*[232]

While these initiatives usually have strong university roots, *Udemy* ('The Academy of You'), a platform where instructors could build courses, publicize them, run them online and manage students, was built by Eren Bali, Oktag Caglar and Gagan Biyani in 2010.[233] Their model was to source high quality instructors and content, and share revenues with the instructors when students paid for these courses. Unacademy, which raised USD 21 million in a Series C funding in July, 2018,[234] is an example from India, which has combined live classes and author driven content as part of its strategy.

*Lynda.com*, started in 1995 by Lynda Weinman, and sold to *LinkedIn* for USD 1.5 billion in 2015,[235] eschewed the formal 'course' experience. Instead of looking at structured courses, they asked knowledge experts to build content in areas such as Web Design, and sold access to the online library at a monthly subscription. Revenues are estimated at over

---

231 About Us, Xuetangx, retrieved on August 5, 2018 from http://www.xuetangx.com/global

232 Pandey, Navadha (2016, July 14). Open online course providers upbeat as enrolments jump, *The Hindu Business Line*, retrieved on July 22, 2018 from https://www.thehindubusinessline.com/news/education/open-online-course-providers-upbeat-as-enrolments-jump/article8850328.ece

233 Udemy, Wikipedia, retrieved on 12 November 2017 from https://en.wikipedia.org/wiki/Udemy

234 Kashyap, Sindhu (2018, July 16), Unacademy raises Series C funding of $21 M led by Sequoia India, SAIF Partners and Nexus Venture Partners, *YourStory*, retrieved on July 22, 2018 from https://yourstory.com/2018/07/unacademy-raises-series-c-funding-21-m-led-sequoia-india-saif-partners-nexus-venture/

235 Porter, Jane (2015, April 27). From near failure to a $1.5 billion sale: The epic story of lynda.com, *FastCompany*, retrieved on 12 November 2017 from https://www.fastcompany.com/3045404/from-near-failure-to-a-15-billion-sale-the-epic-story-of-lyndacom

USD 160 million in 2016.[236] Similar models like *eHow* and *HowStuffWorks* were free to customers and depended on ad revenue to survive. *Pluralsight*, started in 2004 by Aaron Skonnard, Keith Sparkjoy, and Fritz Onion, is estimated to have USD 250 million[237] in revenues in 2016, riding on a subscription model aimed at individuals and corporate and over 5,000 courses. Like *Udacity*,[238] it is already an edTech unicorn at over a billion dollars in valuation. *Simplilearn*, started by Krishna Kumar, aims to be the third edTech company to break past the USD 100 million-revenue mark after *Lynda.com* and *Pluralsight* in the professional education space.

*Coursera* is also experimenting with subscriptions that it launched in 2016,[239] while *Udacity* seems to be moving away from subscriptions and towards an upfront charge broken 'term-wise.'[240] MOOC providers are experimenting big time, both towards and away from the way the traditional systems work, with variations around courses, credentials, financial aid, payment models, industry-connected programs, blended delivery, and cohort size and progression. *Lynda*, *PluralSight* and *Simplilearn* are not strictly MOOC providers, but their practices and profitability are finding more acceptances in the beleaguered MOOC companies that have not yet experienced the benefits of a scalable revenue model.

---

236 Forbes (2016, April 5). Can 'learning paths' boost Linkedin's education revenues?, *Forbes*, retrieved on 12 November 2017 from https://www.forbes.com/sites/greatspeculations/2016/04/05/can-learning-paths-boost-linkedins-education-revenues/#5f9d55a56146

237 Toms, Manu (2017, January 18). Exclusive: Simplilearn to raise $40 mm this year for acquisitions, expansion, *techCircle*, retrieved on 12 November 2017 from http://techcircle.vccircle.com/2017/01/18/exclusive-simplilearn-to-raise-40-mn-this-year-for-acquisitions-expansion/

238 Rao and Primack, (2015, November 11). Online education company Udacity is tech's latest unicorn, *Fortune*, retrieved on 12 November 2017 from http://fortune.com/2015/11/11/udacity-funding/

239 Class Central (2017, November 8). Coursera experiments with a single subscription price for the entire catalog, *Class Central*, retrieved on 12 November 2017 from https://www.class-central.com/report/coursera-specialization-subscription/

240 Shah, Dhawal (2017, October 9). Udacity shifts towards upfront payment without job guarantee, *ClassCentral,* retrieved on 12 November 2017 from https://www.class-central.com/report/udacity-nanodegree-upfront-payment/

In fact, *Udacity* proclaimed MOOCs aren't the way forward because they don't engage students on project-based hands-on training that helps them become ready for careers. *Udacity* Vice President Clarissa Shen said in an interview to The Economic Times in India, 'they are dead… MOOCs are a failed product, at least for the goals we had set for ourselves...Our mission is to bring relevant education which advances people in careers and socio-economic activities, and MOOCs aren't the way,' she told the news daily.[241]

These are not the only companies trying their hands out at making a business out of online learning - many others are making inroads into online learning models and lines between traditional MOOCs and traditional online professional education have blurred already. It is a time when many experiments with student buying and consumption behavior are being carried out to determine what works.

It is also important to note that these experiments have also resulted in the dilution of the initial premise behind these MOOCs – rather than being massive, open, and online, they are being adapted as small, private and blended courses, also called SPOCs (Small Private Online Courses). After all, how massive and open online learning should be handled in terms of pedagogy at scale, not just in terms of content or technology, is not immediately obvious. They are also engineering a shift in the MOOC model from education to training, a less subtle shift, and in that sense moving fast away from their university moorings. By doing so, they are also making them vulnerable to accusations that they will perhaps train, but not be able to educate.

---

241 Young, Jeffrey (2017, October 13). Udacity official declares MOOCs 'dead' (Though the company still offers them), retrieved on 12 November 2017 from https://www.edsurge.com/news/2017-10-12-udacity-official-declares-moocs-dead-though-the-company-still-offers-them

That the move to training will be effective using newer technology, content, and accessibility, is also moot. Nguyen[242] researched studies that compared effectiveness between various delivery formats over the past 100 years or so, 92 percent of which indicated better or similar performance of online learning over traditional education. However, the main conclusion was that it was difficult to say how meaningful these studies really were given the selection bias and the lack of rigorous methodology in these studies. Nguyen proposes that much more rigor has to be brought into future research with a focus on 'self-selection bias, blended instruction, active engagement with the materials, formative assessment, varied materials and repeatable low-stake practice, collaborative learning communities, student maturity, independent learning skills, synchronous and asynchronous work, and student characteristics.' Perhaps personalization and adaptation in the learning and teaching process will provide clearer answers.

That said, there are serious issues at an analytical and conceptual level with the method and design of these courses, which we shall explore here. While they may make money or aspire to, it is not altogether clear that these providers have clear answers on tough questions of pedagogy at scale and effectiveness of online learning. That means that while we forge ahead aggressively, we are also continuing to fail students at an ever increasing scale.

## THE TRUE HISTORY OF MOOCS

**Rewind to October 2008**. Three Canadians, George Siemens, Stephen Downes, and Dave Cormier started the first massive open online course called Connectivism and Connective Knowledge (CCK08) based on a new theory of learning for the digital age called Connectivism, proposed

242 Tuan Nguyen (2015, June). The effectiveness of online learning: beyond no significant difference and future horizons, *MERLOT Journal of Online Learning and Teaching*, Vol. 11, No. 2, retrieved on November 12, 2017 from http://jolt.merlot.org/Vol11no2/Nguyen_0615.pdf

by George Siemens in 2005.[243] Cormier is credited with coining the term 'MOOC' and is also well-known for the theory of Rhizomatic Learning.[244]

MOOCs were created and researched for many years before the current MOOC providers discovered the term. And the term MOOC was not exactly born out of a bottle, with nine audacious ingredients mixed up arbitrarily to create a killer product for higher education.

The founders of the original MOOCs realized that knowledge, society, and technology were experiencing tectonic shifts. They were cognizant of an entire body of work around areas such as OERs, communities of practice (CoPs), networks, the read-write web, open and distance learning, and existing online learning approaches. They brought their own unique ideas to bear upon a framework and theory of how knowledge, learning, and teaching could be interpreted in this digital age.

MOOCs were the product of some extremely deep thinking and research on how learning online could be, at scale. The differences between the original interpretation of the term MOOC and those who used it, starting with *Udacity* in 2011, are so astounding that one is forced to consider the latter having used it for really narrow and subversive needs. The original MOOCs had not only garnered sufficient interest (and critics) in the university circles, but had also gained reputation from the thousands of followers that found them unique and the experience rich. It may not be altogether off the mark to say that there was simply no reason to expropriate the term unless it fitted a grand vision for venture capital – that of an Internet scale sustainable breakthrough, like, say, the next *NetFlix*, or *Twitter*, or *Facebook* – this time in education.

243 Siemens, George (2005, January). Connectivism: A learning theory for the digital age, *International Journal of InstructionTechnology& Distance Learning*, retrieved on November 12, 2017 from http://www.itdl.org/Journal/Jan_05/article01.htm

244 Cormier, Dave (2008). Rhizomatic education: Community as curriculum, *Innovate: Journal of online education*, retrieved on November 12, 2017 from http://nsuworks.nova.edu/cgi/viewcontent.cgi?article=1045&context=innovate

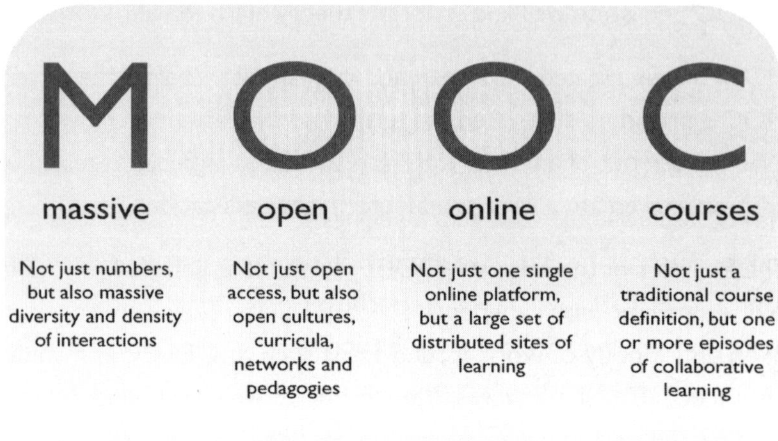


**Figure 22: MOOCs – Expanding the acronym**

The term 'massive' signified the density and richness of interaction in networks of learners, not just their number. While the later MOOCs raced to advertise large numbers, and acquire the most eyeballs, they were not terribly concerned about promoting a new way of learning. It was expeditious for them to take something out of the box and repackage it.

The original MOOCs appreciated the significance of innovating online pedagogy because they understood why traditional elearning had failed. They were concerned about the way people connected to learn, the way networks of learning evolved and in revisiting the nature of online learning. They started using Social Network Analysis (a means of assessing networks in motion, mapping their internal interactions) and looked at measures of connectedness between participants, the value of those interactions to the participants and mechanisms to handle propagation of ideas. They leveraged the idea of Personal Learning Networks (individual and personalized maps of the learning and knowledge networks) and investigated techniques of way-finding and sense-making given the overabundance of information and connections. They researched the importance of strong ties and weak ties within networks, and how they changed over time.

The term 'open' signified not just open access but also a social and cultural openness towards sharing and collaboration in learning and teaching, as well as in its design. It signified a shift in the balance of power between the educators and the educated. Opening up pedagogy, power, structure and progression meant that learners would exhibit a growing degree of control over their own learning. Harnessing networks would mean a greater possibility of meeting and collaborating with people more closely aligned with the way they learned, and a far greater emphasis on trust and reciprocity. It meant a shift from localized learning, to glocalized learning (sparsely knit local and global clusters).[245] Since open access meant diversity, both learners and educators learnt to cope with diverse, sometimes uncharitable opinions, to deal with both encouragement and criticism, and to articulate their reflections properly.

The term 'online' did not indicate just one platform or solution, but a distributed network of 'sites' connected together in the overall narrative of learning and teaching. Rather than expecting everyone to come to 'a' site of learning as the later MOOC providers did to show numbers and control progression, the original MOOCs were spread across multiple sites of interactions – blogs, video channels, social media sites, messaging apps, and even 3D virtual worlds. Some groups even organized in ways that allowed them to meet physically, in smaller numbers. Participants learnt to amplify elements or contributions they liked to their networks and engaged their networks in real life with ideas from the course.

The term 'course' signified an event or an episode of learning, with structure and discourse shaped and formed by the needs of its network,

245 Wellman, Barry (2012). Little boxes, glocalization, and networked individualism, retrieved on April 30, 2019 from http://groups.chass.utoronto.ca/netlab/wp-content/uploads/2012/05/Little-Boxes-Glocalization-and-Networked-Individualism.pdf

and their abilities and interest, not really by the structure of a university course. The progression of the course was parallel and distributed, not sequentially clustered. It wasn't uncommon for discussions of past weeks to still be fresh and referenced by subsequent weeks of focus on different things. It wasn't unknown for some people to drop off for a bit and then resume at the current point and still catch up with what had transpired because others did a great job of summarizing and curating contributions during each week. The 'instructors' of those MOOCs weren't really in control – the participants were actively shaping the discourse. The sheer richness of contributions far outweighed what any curriculum could have designed for, or what any single instructor or team could have moderated or managed in any way.

The original MOOCs were not built with the intention of being monetized or scaled to replace the system of higher education, but they were built to experiment and practice the promise of learning and teaching at scale. They were not focused on credentials or assessments, but more on the nature of teaching and learning in an open and distributed network.

Proposing a new theory of 'learning for the digital age', Connectivism, Siemens asserted the traditional theories of Behaviorism, Cognitivism, and Constructivism could not meet the needs of the current digital age. Rather an altogether new approach, resonant with the growing impact of technology, and new science (like networks and chaos theories), was required. Siemens brought the impact of complexity into education systems. Concepts such as adaptation and self-organization, which dealt with the ability of individuals and networks to negotiate a rapidly shifting world, formed important reference points for proposing the new theory.

Core to the theory of Connectivism is the assertion that *learning is the process of making connections*. These connections could take different forms such as those found in the physical, social, cultural, conceptual or biological networks. These connections shape our learning because they help us navigate the increasing overabundance of information and knowledge, leverage diversity of opinions and build the capacity to know, learn and adapt.

The principles that Siemens proposed celebrated diversity, connection-making, way-finding, sense-making and emphasized the capacity to know more than the actual knowing of something. Connectivism provided the 'insight into learning skills and tasks needed for learners to flourish in a digital era.'

Downes proposed a new definition of knowledge which he called *Connective Knowledge*. He asserted that *knowledge is the network.*[246] He made the assertion that 'at its heart, Connectivism is the thesis that knowledge is distributed across a network of connections and therefore, that learning consists of the ability to construct and traverse those networks' in an intensely personalized and socially interconnected manner, not always expressible by language and its symbols.

Unlike constructivist theories, in Connectivism, knowledge is not thought to be actively constructed.[247] Rather connections form naturally through association and 'knowledge is literally the set of connections formed by actions and experience'. By the same token, knowledge cannot be acquired, built or transferred. The process of learning involves making distributed connections in and across networks. This proposal was a big shift from how knowledge was perceived in other learning theories because if knowledge wasn't a thing or a linguistic entity that could be constructed by the learner or schematized by the teacher for transmission, then most methods we use in learning and teaching today could be questioned for their relevance.

---

246 Downes, Stephen (2007, February 3). What connectivism is, *Half an Hour*, retrieved on November 12, 2017 from http://halfanhour.blogspot.in/2007/02/what-connectivism-is.html

247 Downes, Stephen (2005, December 22). An introduction to connective knowledge, *Half an Hour*, retrieved on November 12, 2017 from http://www.downes.ca/post/33034

## THE FIRST MOOC – CCK08

The first MOOC, CCK08, transformed the way many people, including the author, thought of education and learning. The 12-week course was open and free. Over 2,200 people registered from all over the world.

Even before CCK08 started, participants shaped the curriculum by suggesting areas of personal interest. Each week of the course, facilitators would briefly introduce the topic and suggest relevant open resources. Experts were invited to engage with course participants on each topic followed by an unstructured online conversation. Learning was distributed – participants interacted through tools they were comfortable with (like *Twitter, Facebook, Wordpress and SecondLife*). The facilitators made their network connections and activity public, so that participants could follow the leaders in the field and keep abreast of the latest developments.

Each day, using Downes's *gRSSHopper* technology, participant contributions were harvested from all over the web, important contributions identified and a newsletter sent on to all participants enabling them to keep up with the activity in the course. This newsletter was the prime tool for students to make connections – to ideas and people – that the network threw up.

A few persons (including the author) signed up to become the first paid students in this the first ever MOOC. They submitted three essays that were evaluated directly by the instructors. The final certificate was awarded by the University of Manitoba (the course hosts) at the end of the course. Like many others, the author started a CCK08 Blog[248] that has a collection of posts from each week of the course.

Participants self–organized and formed many virtual and face-to-face open learning networks that outlasted CCK08. They adapted material into their own language and context. The facilitators were always available

248 Baxi, Viplav (2008). CCK08-11 - Viplav Baxi, *Connectivism Meanderings*, retrieved on November 12, 2017 from https://learnoscck08.wordpress.com/

as expert co-learners rather than as instructors. The sheer diversity in the community created tremendously exciting opportunities for learning.

CCK08 also illustrated four key principles of MOOCs – diversity, autonomy, openness, and interactivity. Diversity is reflected in the contributions that people make, leveraging their own perspectives, to the wider network. Autonomy is critical for learners to evaluate choices, ideas and perspectives according to their own needs and goals. Openness is important to ensure that every person is able to move in and out of the learning experience, without impeding boundaries. Interactivity is important from the perspective of learning to 'be' a reflective practitioner as opposed to learning to 'know'. To participate in a MOOC then, would be to engage in a democratic learning experience.[249]

As a result learning 'emerged' rather than being pre-designed. Participants learnt to be practitioners rather than just 'learning to know' or even 'learning to do'. CCK08 also redefined the roles of teachers and students. The role of the teacher as an expert learner was to *model and demonstrate* while the learner had to *practice and reflect.*

Such a learning ecosystem reflects the reality of learning in a digital age, where information is over- abundant, knowledge is increasingly specialized, change is extremely rapid, networks and social media have revolutionized communication, and learning has become largely informal. Such systems of learning can potentially solve the burning problem of employability of our students. It can help them gain the capability to become lifelong learners, acquire 21st century skills and effectively negotiate the rapid shifts in the nature of work. It can raise the quality of teaching and learning significantly, in an equitable and affordable manner.

This thinking is also reflected in the concept of heutagogy – the study of self-determined learning – that, unlike pedagogy and andragogy, marks

249 Downes, Stephen (2010, October 22). What is democracy in education, *Half an Hour*, retrieved on November 13, 2017 from http://www.downes.ca/post/54025

a significant move away from traditional teacher-centered learning. Heutagogy extends the popular theory of andragogy or self-directed learning by focusing on 'capability.' Capable people are those who 'know how to learn; are creative; have a high degree of self-efficacy; can apply competencies in novel as well as familiar situations; and can work well with others.'[250]

Since 2008, there have been a large number of MOOCs on the lines of CCK08. These MOOCs such as the *Future of Education, Critical Literacies, Change 11* and other versions of CCK itself, have seen rich interaction globally. A lot of published research and a strong community of educators, theorists, developers and thought-leaders have emerged. There have been critics too.[251] They questioned whether Connectivism could be rightfully called a theory of learning or if it was just a combination of many ideas put together in an instructional framework intended to guide teaching and learning in a digital age. Downes[252] and Siemens have argued that it presents an altogether new vocabulary to describe learning and stands up as a theory in its own right. It isn't a debate that has decisive answers for now.

## RHIZOMATIC LEARNING

Cormier evolved the concept of Rhizomatic Learning[253] on the basis of which he has grown the Rhizo-MOOC.

---

250 Hase, Stewart and Chris Kenyon, (2000). From Andragogy to Heutagogy, retrieved on April 30, 2019 from http://pandora.nla.gov.au/nph-wb/20010220130000/http://ultibase.rmit.edu.au/Articles/dec00/hase2.htm

251 Wade, M.C. (2012, May 30). A critique of connectivism as a learning theory, *cybergouge*, retrieved on November 12, 2017 from http://cybergogue.blogspot.in/2012/05/critique-of-connectivism-as-learning.html

252 Downes, Stephen (2014, April 21). Connectivism as learning theory, *Half an Hour*, retrieved on November 12, 2017 from http://halfanhour.blogspot.in/2014/04/connectivism-as-learning-theory.html

253 Cormier, Dave (2008, June 3). Rhizomatic education: community as curriculum, retrieved on November 12, 2017 from http://davecormier.com/edblog/2008/06/03/rhizomatic-education-community-as-curriculum/

> A rhizomatic plant has no center and no defined boundary; rather, it is made up of a number of semi-independent nodes, each of which is capable of growing and spreading on its own, bounded only by the limits of its habitat.

Cormier described a learning experience similar to a rhizome wherein learning itself is organic and emergent, deeply driven by personal context, flexible boundaries, and multiple pathways. Rhizomatic teaching, in turn, describes a teaching experience that sets the context, facilitates the inter-connections of ideas through conversations, and empowers the community to engineer its own curriculum.

Rhizomatic Learning builds up the core capability to learn in a distributed learning environment. It leverages all the attendant benefits of network-led and community-based learning, but distinguishes itself by describing a personal 'self-reproducing' capability to learn. The agency to learn rests with the learner and the learning community she is part of. The agency to teach is distributed among all the learners, who really establish the curriculum. The resultant is messy and complex, with individual outcomes possibly far in deviation to any expected outcomes from the community.

In Rhizomatic Learning, the definition of a course veers away from the traditional. It is a sense of time-bound evented-ness, a shared context which aggregates a community. Its curriculum is formed by the community, which evolves and extends it continuously through prior knowledge and emergent opinions. It may engender several artistic and creative forms of expression, not necessarily formal artifacts associated with traditional courses.

Rhizomatic Learning is characterized by *learning freedom*. It draws heavily upon openness, lack of centralized control, autonomy, diversity and interaction. Freedom in learning drives most of the interactions, liberating the learning experience.

In contrast, connectivist models uphold 'connection-making' as the primary source of learning and knowledge. There is connection-making in Rhizomatic Learning, but that is merely a medium. The focus is on free, unrestricted sharing and unpredictable pathways in learning. In that sense, the *afterthought* focus on *Critical Literacies*[254] in the connectivist MOOCs, becomes the starting point for Rhizomatic Learning. What is 'tidy' in the network model, becomes messy in the rhizomatic one. The replication of learning capability in distributed environments is key – the 'more of how you can learn, is learning' of Rhizomatic Learning overwhelms the 'those that have, get' rules of networks. In that sense, Rhizomatic Learning deliberately empowers personalized learning.

## xMOOCS AND cMOOCS

The MOOCs as originally envisioned, meant questioning the existing paradigm from the perspective of a digital age, scale, and effectiveness. Downes puts it succinctly when he says:[255]

> MOOCs were not designed to serve the missions of the elite colleges and universities. They were designed to undermine them, and make those missions obsolete. Yes there has been a great rebranding and co-option of the concept of the MOOC over the last couple of years. The near-instant response from the elites, almost unprecedented in my experience, is a recognition of the deeply subversive intent and design of the original MOOCs (which they would like very much to erase from history).

254 Downes, Stephen (2015, October 30). Critical literacies and the challenge of online learning, retrieved on November 13, 2017 from http://www.downes.ca/presentation/369; The Critical Literacies MOOC investigated the literacies we need to have in a digital learning environment. See also Steve Mackenzie - http://learnadoodledastic.blogspot.in/2010/06/critical-literacy-course-online.html

255 Downes, Stephen (2013, April 13). The great rebranding, *Half an Hour,* retrieved on November 12, 2017 from http://halfanhour.blogspot.in/2013/04/the-great-rebranding.html

Siemens summarized his interpretation of the difference between the original MOOCs and the new ones by stating,[256] '...there is overlap between our model and that of *Coursera/EDx*. However, *Coursera/EDx* emulates the existing education system, choosing instead to *transfer* it online rather than *transform* it online'.

To distinguish between the two, Downes termed the original MOOCs 'cMOOCs' (for Connectivist MOOCs) and the newer ones as 'xMOOCs', the 'x' standing for being an extension of something else. That something else was really the type of eLearning that had grown very rapidly since the late 1990s. Corporations and even online learning providers found it expedient to digitize expensive face to face training and create standardized, mass learning experiences for their employees, in order to cut costs and save working time that was lost in training and travel.

Siemens also distinguishes further between these two. He makes the point that in cMOOCs, coherence is 'learner formed and instructor guided.' Learners make sense and find their way through the interactions in a network. At times they synchronize or harmonize, not solely to the demands of the instructor, but also with learners and the state of 'knowledge' in the network. In the xMOOCs, however, instructors are at the core, the curriculum mercilessly harmonizes instruction, and learners operate in narrow groups rather than as connective networks or communities of practice.

For the most part, the xMOOCs tried to simply replicate the traditional classroom and curricular practices online. In traditional online learning, all learning is centrally directed, restricted to the closed boundaries of the course, performed generally alone (collaboration features exhibit very low usage patterns), mass personalized with rigid pre-determined learning paths and assessed largely through objective type assessments.

---

256 Siemens, George (2012, June 6). What is the theory that underpins our MOOCs, retrieved on 22 July, 2018 from http://www.elearnspace.org/blog/2012/06/03/what-is-the-theory-that-underpins-our-moocs/

This type of eLearning had already failed to scale for many reasons. It was designed for stereotypes of industrial age learners. It ignored the diversity and overabundance of information that is present in real life. It ignored the autonomy of learners who needed to personalize the learning experience. It ignored the richness of interaction on the World Wide Web. It did not empower learners with the agency and choice it needed in setting the curricular agenda. It ignored the 'conversation' and 'connections' in learning. xMOOCs are extensions of this type of eLearning.

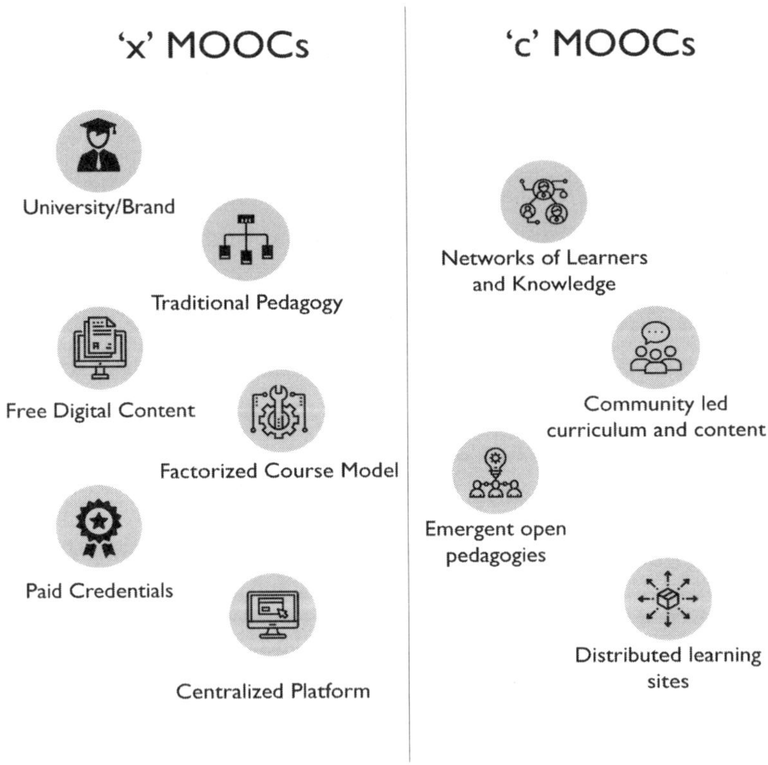


**Figure 23: Distinguishing between xMOOCs and cMOOCs**

By only incrementally extending this type of online learning, xMOOCs have massively magnified challenges such as low retention, rote learning, low employability, and lack of student ownership, motivation, interactivity, and engagement. It is as if they have ignored more than two decades of insights from online, open, and distance education.

There are two key challenges facing the xMOOCs. First, the pedagogy behind these xMOOCs needs a rethink. They have adopted the title MOOC but ignored the rich underlying connectivist origins. They have merely extended traditional online, instructivist Web Based Training (WBT) and Instructor Led Training (ILT) methods to a massive audience.

WBTs and ILTs were designed as eLearning equivalents, of expensive classroom training, to reduce training delivery costs and standardize instruction for large scale corporate training. But nearly everyone realizes that this type of eLearning is not scalable because it is designed for learner stereotypes, does not account for real world diversity and in general, predates and ignores the entire social learning revolution. A WBT is usually to be consumed in an isolated self-paced manner and is directed at a specific perception of who the target of this mass produced course is.

Both for WBTs/ILTs and xMOOCs, the model is largely teacher (and/or instructional designer) led and content-driven. It not based upon socially negotiated, digitally mediated and distributed learning, the hallmark of the cMOOCs. This is why it is perhaps more appropriate to call them XBTs (or 'massive' extensions of WBTs and ILTs) rather than think of them as a variant of the original MOOC approach.

The XBTs augment the traditional systems, giving importance to institutional pedigree, clearly defined institutional structures and processes (such as courses, terms and exams) and certification mechanisms. XBTs are closed, insular micro-systems of learning, replicating the scholastic structure of the classroom and the administrative structure of the qualification or degree, to an approximate online form.

The connectivist MOOCs are very open, emphasize sense-making, operate in a distributed fashion, legitimize learners at the periphery (legitimate peripheral participation or 'lurking') and do not impose the strict conformance to traditional notions of course, exam, and certification. For them, since learning is the process of making connections and knowledge is the network, the competency and capability to learn, critically determines the learning itself.

The cMOOC platforms enable the conversation by aggregating the member contributions, making them accessible by remixing and repurposing them in forms that are useful to search/consume and feeding them forward to members. This mechanism results in the course progressing into areas not anticipated when the cMOOC was conceptualized. In this sense, learning becomes an emergent phenomenon with ever changing contours. And learners learn to adapt to these dynamic conditions and to self-organize in ways that are meaningful to them. This is what happens in real life as we learn and evolve. This is not very helpful as a design for replication for planners who, as you could well imagine, cannot operate in such apparently dynamic environments.

Secondly, engagement and retention are key aspects of the learning experience that the MOOCs, in general, have not been able to address effectively. The long tail of learning, which is that a really large number of learners end up not completing the MOOC or remain at low levels of engagement, is nothing new. It is just that the massive nature of MOOCs amplifies some of these known issues.

It is here that the MOOC providers need to spend a lot of time experimenting with techniques such as gamification, badges, adaptive learning, and learning analytics. At scale, many new ways of analyzing and predicting the behavior of networked learners, have emerged. Analysis of learning 'trails' or records of learner behavior over time, can help predict, for example, students at-risk of failure. They can help educators and learners equally through actionable insights.

The Connectivist model relies on learners to build capability for their own learning, something that is the desired endgame for any educational system. By increasing learner capability to learn in the digital medium, cMOOCs can potentially flatten the long tail. Learner capability can be built if we build mechanisms for empowering learners, make learning increasingly more open so that diverse influences may be experienced, and encourage opportunities for collaborative reflection within and outside the learning process. The traditional xMOOC models can instead only reinforce and amplify the long tail, by encouraging ambiguous online learning practices at a very large scale.

Both the xMOOC and the cMOOC approaches will need a lot of experimentation and innovation. And they will yield better results because learners will be better connected and more in control of their learning. MOOCs could work if better understood at scale and research should be intensified to achieve this outcome. If MOOCs could really be made to work at scale, we would have solved a large and important challenge facing education today.

# #11

# What*If*

## school was not school?

# #11 WHAT*IF* SCHOOL WAS NOT SCHOOL?

*Or at least not as we traditionally know it.*

*What if schools were owned and managed very differently? What if teachers or parents formed a cooperative to run the school? How would they manage both administration and teaching? Would they be more responsive to local needs?*

*What if teachers were made part owners of schools? Would these schools be sustainable without backing from philanthropists, private capital, or political muscle? How would they work with educational boards or district administration when required to? What if the cooperative model was really successful and scalable as in other sectors?*

You know a school to be a central place where students, teachers, and staff assemble together every day. Infrastructure such as rooms, playgrounds, and labs are created for specific purposes. Equipment and materials are procured and deployed at the school. Students come to this central place to learn. Teachers come to this central place to teach. The schools are led by administrators who appoint teachers and manage the school operations, its funds, and its growth and improvement over time. The administrators are appointed by school trusts or public departments of education, who are each in turn funded privately or by the government. Private tuition teachers and coaching centers thrive in after-school hours, fuelled by either the need for better education or the need to pass examinations, a parallel classroom system in its own right. These are the building blocks of the school system.

What if we were to question some of these building blocks? For example, what if teachers and parents formed cooperatives to run schools instead of private trusts and government departments? Do we really need an 'educracy' to manage the school construct? What value do specialized administrators really add? Each of these questions may be incongruous or uncomfortable to consider, after all 'educratic' schools are an efficient construct, at least they are thought to be so.

## SCHOOLS AS COOPERATIVES

So let us for a moment imagine a future where schools are run by teachers' cooperatives. That is, instead of an administrative and financial superstructure of wealthy philanthropists or businesspersons or trusts, political muscle, 'educratic' leadership and all the trappings of modern world schools, teachers would cooperate to teach, learn, and administer the school.

Or let us consider a case where parents form the school ownership, with support from local communities and teachers. Parents are definitely more vested in their children's future, but on the other hand, teaching and administering schools is a full-time job, which requires specialized professional knowledge as well.

The Amul cooperative in India,[257] formed in 1946 in the western state of Gujarat in India, demonstrated a model for cooperatives in the dairy sector. In those days, a cartel operated that controlled the supply chain. With the power of acting as the intermediary between the farmer and the market, the cartel engaged in exploitative practices. Helped by prominent freedom fighters like Sardar Patel, the farmers decided to wrest control from the middlemen, and manage their own procurement, processing, marketing, and distribution. The farmers co-owned the dairies, and elected representatives and professionals to manage the dairies, village societies, district unions, and the federation of unions. In 1965, the then Prime Minister Lal Bahadur Shastri decided this approach would form the basis for the National Dairy Development Policy. Today, more than 15 million milk producers supply milk to about 150,000 dairy societies, which belong to 184 district unions, that are marketed by 22 state marketing federations, directly to the end customers. India is the largest milk producer in the world. Amul had three million milk producers and revenues of over USD 2 billion in 2012.[258] In short, the cooperative model works at scale, is the basis of national policy, and has catapulted India to the forefront of milk production.

OK. So what has that got to do with education? After all, producing milk and educating the next generation are completely different things. Interestingly enough, the cooperative model is not new to education. Avalon, New Country School, SUPAR, and Woodland Park are examples from the US.

---

257 About Us - The Amul Model, retrieved on April 30, 2019 from https://amul.com/m/about-us

258 Triple Pundit (2012, October 16). How Amul turned India into the world's largest milk producer – sustainably, *Triple Pundit*, retrieved on November 19, 2017 from https://www.triplepundit.com/2012/10/amul-sustainability-india/

In 1994, the first teacher cooperative based school, Minnesota New Country School (MNCS),[259] was formed as a collaboration between *EdVisions*, a teachers' cooperative, and the local school district.[260] In 2002, it was called the 'coolest' school in America. *EdVisions's* idea was to build an enterprise of teachers, just like you would establish 'a law firm or medical practice'. The enterprise would then offer instructional programs that schools would sign up for.

> EdVisions Co-op replaces union arrangements by creating a professional association of teachers and owners that contract with a school board to supply a learning program.

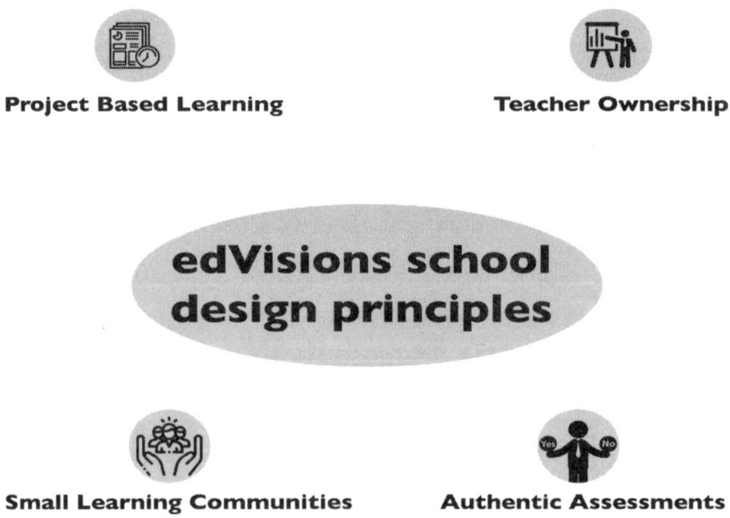


**Figure 24: The EdVisions design principles**

As a corporation formed to operate teacher cooperatives, *EdVisions* took on the mandate to operate charter schools from any of the charter boards in Minnesota. They allocated a group of teachers from

259 New Country School, retrieved on November 20, 2017 from https://newcountryschool.com/

260 Our History, EdVisions Cooperative, retrieved on April 30, 2019 from http://edvisionscooperative.org/about/history/

the cooperative, a 'site team', to make decisions about the curriculum, budgets, and personnel. The site team paid *EdVisions* an administrative fee for managing payroll and benefits. The *EdVisions* model had teachers as owners in its initial vision, but that did not work out as planned. Now it is a professional development, personnel, and payroll services organization servicing 12 schools in Minnesota and 35 schools nationwide.

The school design principles that *EdVisions* followed were really interesting.

First, the traditional curricular approach was discarded and project based learning became the norm. With this approach, 'students literally design their own education as they brainstorm, design, and execute independent, student-initiated projects.'[261]

The second principle of the *EdVisions* school design was based around *small learning communities.*[262] These are groups of teachers clustered around one or more areas, and mentoring a group of students, typically breaking departmental and class-section silos. They could take the form of a school-within-a-school (for example, school of business and technology or school of law, government and public service), academies (formed around a curricular theme such as humanities), career pathways (usually a 3-4 year structure with a work or career focus across the curriculum) or multi-grade or single-grade clusters of students. The strategies employed by such schools include flexible use of time (like block scheduling), reducing the student-teacher ratio through techniques such as alternate scheduling, extending the classroom to the workplace, and personalizing learning.

---

261 What Is Project-Based Learning?, Avalon School, retrieved on November 21, 2017 from http://www.avalonschool.org/pbl

262 Allen, Lili, Cheryl Almeida and Adria Steinberg. Wall to Wall: Implementing small learning communities in five Boston high schools, Northeast and Islands Regional Educational Laboratory, Brown University, retrieved on November 20, 2017 from https://www.brown.edu/academics/education-alliance/sites/brown.edu.academics.education-alliance/files/publications/Wall2Wall.pdf

The third principle was centered on authentic assessment.[263] Authentic assessments are used to derive a better understanding of student competencies and strengths (not gaps) as they are based on representative challenges in a given discipline. They contain ill-structured and sometimes ambiguous problem statements that need critical thinking skills to structure and refine. They are designed on a wider bank of knowledge and skills than that for traditional assessments. They may contain a hands-on real life demonstration, but are equally well-suited for abstract subjects or concepts that are not manifested in the real world.

The fourth principle was teacher ownership. Instead of having a hierarchical structure with the teacher having little effective say in school operations, curricula, and methods, cooperative-led schools put teachers in charge.

Various schools have implemented these four principles to a greater or lesser degree. A variant of the *Edvisions* approach, the Avalon Charter School is an independent public charter established in 2000 in Minnesota, US, run entirely by parents, students and teachers.[264] This school is entirely governed by its teachers, and 'staff members assume administrative duties and have equal authority in all decision-making situations.' Decisions are made through a 'fist of five' method with a closed fist denoting complete disagreement and an open hand indicating complete agreement with a decision. They set their own salary scales and make decisions about the budget for the school. In the process, they determine what is working or not, and have the autonomy to change something that is not working. They learn a host of new skills in both teaching and non-teaching areas and are able to bring their skills into shared use. Teachers like their freedom and attrition is very low. They perform a 360 degree evaluation where teachers, students, and leadership teams provide feedback on one another.

---

263 Wiggins, Grant (2013). 27 characteristics of authentic assessment, *TeachThought*, retrieved on April 30, 2019 from https://www.teachthought.com/pedagogy/27-characteristics-of-authentic-assessment/

264 About Us, Avalon Charter School, retrieved on November 19, 2017 from http://www.avalonschool.org/about-us/our-history

Teachers empower students to take responsibility for school governance and mediate with peers. Students are encouraged to find their own meta-cognitive space, learning to learn,[265] a skill that takes time to build - 'sometimes two years before a student understands that success is primarily a function of what they put into it as opposed to how well they play by someone's rules.' The student transforms from an 'object of instruction' to the role of a primary agent in the education system. Some fail, only to really appreciate the true purpose of their education. Project based learning is the norm at Avalon and students are expected to grade their own projects on the basis of a given guideline. All senior projects require a public presentation.

Avalon has a student Congress which makes all decisions using a constitution they themselves wrote as part of a class project. They can make any laws pertaining to the students and the student/advisor (teacher) relationship within the confines of their constitution. For example, when all high schools had been struggling with the use of cellphones by students, the Avalon Congress decided it wasn't going to ban them. They realized that it was not the cellphone, but the persistent disruption to class that was the problem. So they passed a law penalizing the student who was found disrupting the class by misusing the cellphone. Students also lay down the rules for how they should treat each other and their advisors, and how they should mediate unruly behavior. This is real democratic schooling, with the student voice an important part of the equation.

Parents and the wider community play an important role. They act as assistants to teachers, help in organizing school activities, provide expertise and resources, and take far greater control over their child's learning. They can also hold teachers accountable for performance outcomes or standards.

---

265 Kerchner, Charles Taylor (2010). Can teachers run their own schools? Tales from the islands of teacher cooperatives, retrieved on November 19, 2017 from http://charlestkerchner.com/cr/uploadImages/Teacher_run_case.pdf

Project Based Learning at Avalon breaks the traditional structured classes and grade levels organization structure, just like at MNCS. There are no small learning communities, but there is emphasis on elements like individualized learning plans, authentic activities, lower student to teacher ratios and multi-age advisories.

Some questions really bothered the initial group of teachers. As they scaled, would they still be able to make group decisions, rather than breaking down into smaller groups? Would their school graduates be able to take the next step in their careers? Would they be financially sustainable? The fact that they are financially solid, that they have emerged stronger through the test of time, and that they still retain the energy to go forward after nearly two decades of operations is a testament to the fact that what they started has worked.

It is interesting to note that Minnesota has been organizing agricultural business through cooperatives for generations. Perhaps this is why the idea of a teacher cooperative or a teacher empowered governance model found resonance in the state. This model 'challenges both the notion of ownership and that of bureaucratic management.' It is important to note that the exact shape and form for these cooperatives is not something that is designed from the top down. Rather it is emergent, based on the dynamics of the people, context, and tools.

The Milwaukee teacher-run schools have been greatly inspired by the work of Cris Parr and John Parr, who visited the Minnesota *EdVisions* schools and made one significant change. They did not believe that the teachers needed to take economic risks. They mediated an agreement between the district and the teachers union under which teacher-run schools could be established and teachers could be employed and paid by the district instead of having to fend for their own. The Parrs established the School for Urban Planning and Architecture, or SUPAR, on these lines.

The Centre for Learning (CFL), Bengaluru, India, was formed in 1990 and is completely teacher-run without the usual hierarchy.[266] It is inspired by the work of J Krishnamurti, one of the greatest thinkers and religious teachers of all time.[267] Parents form an important part of the teaching and learning process at CFL. The teachers operate in a democratic manner, with voting rights on every decision on an equal footing. They organize themselves in small and large groups based on the area of operation and the competency required.

## PARENTS AS SCHOOL OWNERS

In another case, at the Woodland Park Cooperative School,[268] parents cooperatively own the school, hire professional teachers, and assist them actively in both academic and administrative chores. Parents can earn credits for completing educational programs that make them better parents and support to teachers. This is a pre-primary school, as opposed to the earlier examples where these models have been applied from Grade six onwards.

In India, there are examples of parents getting together to start a school. The Bombay International School, Mumbai, was conceived over a waffle party of expatriate and Indian mothers in 1961.[269] They did not want their children to go through 'academic pressure, punishment, and rote learning.' Illustrious parents like artist M F Hussain and physicist Dr. Raja Ramanna joined the initiative. They now follow the International Baccalaureate (IB) program which emphasizes real-life project based learning approaches and the more traditional Indian Schools Certifi-

---

266 Centre for Learning, retrieved on November 23, 2017 from https://cfl.in/

267 An overview of Krishnamurti's life and work, retrieved on November 23, 2017 from http://www.jkrishnamurti.org/about-krishnamurti/biography.php

268 Hobson, Tom (2011). Cooperative nuts and bolts: How our school works, retrieved on November 21, 2017 from http://teachertomsblog.blogspot.in/2011/08/cooperative-nuts-and-bolts-how-our.html

269 The Bombay International School, About, retrieved on November 23, 2017 from http://bisschool.com/history/

cate Examinations (ICSE) board. Like this school, there are many other schools in India such as the Citizens Gurukul School[270] and the Indus Early Learning Centre that are also parent-led.[271]

Waldorf or Steiner education[272] has also impacted many schools worldwide. In India, there are many Waldorf schools, controlled and run by parents looking for an alternative system of education for their children. The Waldorf model of education is based on the work of Rudolph Steiner (1861-1925) in the early 20th century. One of the really interesting aspects of the Waldorf education model is that students construct their own lesson book and projects. The teacher, trained in the Waldorf methods, is responsible for initiating and immersing the student into a topic by way of stories, recitations, performing arts, writing and reading. The students go through the topic in increasing horizontal and vertical subject depth. The teacher has the freedom to adjust pedagogy and scheduling to meet the student learning needs and natural rhythms.[273]

Are these models truly scalable? One would like to believe that this could be the case, given the history of cooperative movements like Amul. It requires shedding of traditional forms of control, the passion of and commitment from stakeholders, and policy driven support. Ownership patterns, funding mechanisms, teacher development, school mentoring and many other critical components of this changed ownership will need to be closely looked at. Pedagogy invariably suffers at scale, so an informed decentralized approach to both teaching and learning, is a necessary corollary.

---

270 Bhat, Avinash (2018, July 01). Citizens Gurukul shuts down as no students turn up for admission, *New Indian Express*, retrieved on April 29, 2019 from http://www.newindianexpress.com/cities/bengaluru/2018/jul/01/citizens-gurukul-shuts-down-as-no-students-turn-up-for-admission-1836434.html

271 Saran, Shweta (2017, June 3). When parents step in to run schools, *LiveMint*, retrieved on April 30, 2019 from http://www.livemint.com/Sundayapp/QMpg7zZBbYCQYYh5GiIGfK/When-parents-step-in-to-run-schools.html

272 Waldorf Answers, retrieved on November 23, 2017 from http://www.waldorfanswers.org/RudolfSteiner.htm

273 TRESD (2006). What is a Waldorf Methods Education?, *TRESD*, retrieved on April 30, 2019 from http://web.archive.org/web/20070211092340/http://www.tresd.k12.ca.us/waldorf.html

There is merit in discussing these models if they lead to increased stakeholder trust and respect, higher quality learning, diversity, and autonomy. What if there were a significant proportion of cooperative schools in India catering to local needs, responsive to the local community, and creating environments where students could really take responsibility for their own learning? Such cooperatives could be served by other cooperatives as well – for needs ranging from administrative/professional services to needs such as teacher education and leadership development. The thought is not to replace traditional schools, but to enable teacher and parent run schools to thrive and demonstrate viability at scale, supported by policy.

# #12

# What*If*
## teachers made students laugh?

# #12 WHAT*IF* TEACHERS MADE STUDENTS LAUGH?

*Laughter increases student engagement and has a positive effect on learning outcomes. It builds trust and removes fear.*

*What if we used humor as a strategic tool in our classrooms? What if we promoted constructive forms of humor in our classrooms? What if we could relieve student stress through more humor?*

*What if we were able to explain concepts better through humor? What if we were able to build critical skills of tolerance and the ability to take criticism using humor?*

Laughter increases engagement, confidence, and builds comfort and trust. It positively impacts both learning and teaching. Laughter signifies play, and play helps learning. It beats stress and improves memory. It breaks down the barriers of socialization. It helps nervous teachers settle down in a new class. Laughter creates a positive classroom environment and has been shown to improve class management. It has also been seen to increase attention and level of concentration. Humor can also be directly used to enhance learning.

What if we had more humor in the classroom? What if teachers learnt how to use humor appropriately? What if humor was used as a technique to break monotony, remove fear and increase learning? After all, the difference between 'HAHA' and the 'AHA' is the 'H' for humor.[274]

One of my favorite humorous encounters in the classroom occurred in my statistics class. The joke the teacher told us went like this:

> Surgeon: Only one in every ten patients on an average that I treat has a surgical complication.
>
> Patient: That sounds cool. How many patients have you treated before me who haven't faced any complications?
>
> Surgeon: Nine.

Depending on averages for prediction is problematic. Just using averages, we cannot predict what is going to happen next. Then how can we predict what could happen in the future? A simple humorous example, in context of the learning, led us to curiously explore various probability functions and models of prediction. It engaged us in a meaningful search for a solution to the patient's problem. And we enjoyed engaging in that search.

---

274 Curtis, Susan (2016, March 16). Humor in the classroom, retrieved on November 19, 2017 from https://www.middleweb.com/5053/humor-in-the-classroom/ HAHA and AHA – the connection is made by Joel Goodman, an educator.

Not all statistics professors may be able to do what Ron Berk (who considers 'humor as an instructional defibrillator', and has a book with that phrase in the title) did with his class, though.

> In his course, Berk stages lavish, over-the-top musical skits - starring him and students - that draw from pop culture. In one spoof, 'All That Jazz' blares as several students wearing white gloves saunter into the room. Their hands flare and bodies contort into isolated movements in time with the music. Suddenly the music and dancers stop. Abruptly the theme from 'Rocky,' blasts out of the speakers, and a horde of students in hooded sweatshirts barge into the classroom, throwing punches in the air. Students gawk and laugh at the spectacle, while Berk illustrates the concept of statistical sampling designs by discussing how students were selected for the two groups and detaching the similarities and differences in the group's compositions.

## THE THEORY OF INSTRUCTIONAL HUMOR

It stands to reason. Being able to 'see' humor in a serious and difficult learning situation not only relieves the stress but can also provide a serious learning perspective. In one study of an English learning classroom,[275] results revealed 'significant difference on test scores measuring recall between classes with humor and classes without humor.' Retention of more challenging materials was higher in classes where humor was applied. Students exhibited better recall in tests conducted six to nine weeks later. When considering humor vs. the level of difficulty of the material in this English language class setting, '86 percent of difficult semantic concepts were made easier by the use of humor, 90 percent of difficult vocabulary items became easier and 74 percent of difficult vocabulary concepts became easier with humor.' It was also found that students like more humor if the material is more difficult.

---

275 Aboudan, Rima (2009). Laugh and learn: humor and learning a second language, *International Journal of Arts and Sciences,* 3(3): 90 - 99 ISSN: 1944-6934 retrieved on August 05, 2018 from https://pdfs.semanticscholar.org/4fac/36fe76826917bd338c60195e1a616a6bbbf1.pdf

A sense of humor, a funny bone, is really important in a teacher. A teacher must be able to spot humor, create situations of humor and use it judiciously while teaching. Humorous teachers use quotations, anecdotes, games, play-acting, facial expressions, quips, physical movements, sound and many other things to create humorous situations. They use doodles, cartoons, music, and many other elements to bring in an additional amount of humor in their classrooms.

But humor can often turn sour. It could be ill-timed, irrelevant, or poorly executed. It could also be overdone. Destructive humor could be disastrous. It could be insensitively directed at someone (ridicule), it could divide and exclude, and it may offend.

> In other words, humor directed at a student in the form of ridicule, sarcasm, and joking references to ethnic, racial, and gender differences are out, say experts.[276]

Constructive humor involves rather than excludes, builds an atmosphere of caring rather than breaking confidence, and invites positive repartee rather than aggressive and combative retorts.

> Humor, used appropriately, can help reduce the psychological distance between teachers and students, while inappropriate humor increases distance.[277]

Comedians will tell you that enacting humor is an art. They understand how difficult it is to be humorous.

For many teachers, laughter and humor may indeed be a real challenge that they would need help with. Perhaps over time, they would be able to discover their funny bone. But they would still have to study the art and practice it, not to become the class comedians, but to be able to extract just enough of this art to become more effective teachers.

---

276 Education update (2001). Make me laugh – using humor in the classroom, ***Education Update***, August 2001, Volume 43, No. 5, retrieved on November 16, 2017 from http://www.ascd.org/publications/newsletters/education-update/aug01/vol43/num05/Make-Me-Laugh.aspx

277 Ibid

Humor outside the actual transaction of teaching and learning, but still inside the classroom or school, can also be very effective. Teachers can use humor effectively in these situations, personalized to the way a student or a group of students behave in class. Here is an interesting story from Chad Donohue,[278] a middle school English and social studies teacher.

Donohue had a 13-year old student who usually had a very somber demeanor. During an exam, he walked up to Donohue, all very seriously, and in hushed tones, asked for a little piece of paper to finish his essay. Donohue, equally seriously, asked him if he was sure he really wanted a little piece of paper. The student was a little confused by the question, but said yes. Then Donohue took a sheet of paper and tore off a little piece to give to the student.

> 'I think I need a whole sheet,' he said, grinning.
>
> I looked cautiously concerned and said, 'Well, I'm sure you know what you're doing.'
>
> He was caught off guard by this exchange, but he was also tickled. In fact, it fueled his participation for the remainder of the period and brought his stress levels down. He is a very serious student who is concerned with performing well on everything. In my classroom, however, he isn't afraid to make a mistake. He knows it's going to be okay.

This example brings out the fact that every student responds differently to humor. The serious student was stressed about his essay and probably worried that he had to cover more ideas in his essay than he had the sheets for. Donohue made him ease up a bit, not to detract from his seriousness or to make fun of it, but to make him appreciate that it is important to stay relaxed while working on serious things.

278 Donohue, Chad (2014, May 20). Laughing in the classroom-safely, retrieved on November 19, 2017 from https://www.tolerance.org/magazine/laughing-in-the-classroomsafely

It is important to appreciate that not all children start out with the same level of stress. For most children, their life outside the classroom, in general or on that particular day, contributes to their level of stress. School often compounds it. This stress affects the quality of their learning.

Teachers are human too, and subject to many adult stresses. Sometimes their stress levels are reflected in the way they teach and how they engage with their class. A humorous teacher learns to use humor to deal with her own stress as well so that her students learn in a positive class environment.

> The whole object of comedy is to be yourself, and the closer you get to that, the funnier you'll be. (Jerry Seinfeld.[279])

Humorous teachers understand another really important thing – laughing at themselves is as important as laughing with others.[280] When exhibited in a class or group, laughing at oneself is a transferable attribute. Students may appreciate that attitude and become more tolerant. They may also learn to be more discerning of the destructive types of humor and consciously refrain from them. They may also discover and express their funny bone, adding to the engagement in the classroom.

## EVIDENCE THAT HUMOR WORKS

A summary report of four decades of research on instructional humor consolidates theories that underpin humor and its use, as well as various classifications.[281]

---

279 Stephenson, Sue (2014, December 3). Ha! Ha! Building Serious Skills Using Stand-Up Comedy, retrieved on November 19 from https:/www.middleweb.com/14010/ha-ha-building-serious-skills-using-stand- comedy/

280 Strean, William (2008). Evolving toward laughter in learning: Collected essays on learning and teaching. 1. 10.22329/celt.v1i0.3182, retrieved on November 19 from https://www.researchgate.net/publication/268180988_Evolving_Toward_Laughter_in_Learning

281 Banas, John. A., Norah Dunbar; Dariela Rodriguez; Shr-Jie Liu, (2010, December 10). A review of humor in educational settings: four decades of research, retrieved on April 30, 2019 from https://www.tandfonline.com/doi/abs/10.1080/03634523.2010.496867

The Instructional Humor Processing Theory[282] (IHPT) is an important integrative theory to explain the role humor plays in an instructional setting. IHPT considers the ability of the students to appreciate humor as a key parameter of instructional effectiveness of humor.

> According to the IHPT, for humor to facilitate learning, students need to perceive and then resolve the incongruity in a humorous instructional message. If the students do not resolve the incongruity, they may experience confusion instead of humor. Further, the IHPT proposes that the recognition of humor will increase students' attention.

As an example of classificatory research, one preliminary study[283] was conducted to identify types of humor that are appropriate or inappropriate in the classroom. The researchers enumerated as many as 41 types of humor and classified them into four categories each of appropriate and inappropriate humor, based on 712 (appropriate) and 513 (inappropriate) examples of teacher humor respectively.

Appropriate humor included categories such as humor related to the course or unrelated to it, humor that was self-disparaging and unintentional humor. Inappropriate humor included categories such as offensive humor, disparaging humor directed at a student or at something or someone else, and self-disparaging humor that was belittling in nature. Nearly half (47 percent) of the examples fell into the first category – teacher humor linked to the course materials. Four subcategories - media/external objects (19 percent), jokes (14 percent), examples (14 percent), and stories (13 percent) - comprised 60 percent of this category.

---

282 Wanzer, Melissa Bekelja & Ann Bainbridge Frymier (2010, January). An explanation of the relationship between instructor humor and student learning: instructional humor processing theory, retrieved on April 30, 2019 from https://www.researchgate.net/publication/248940257_An_Explanation_of_the_Relationship_between_Instructor_Humor_and_Student_Learning_Instructional_Humor_Processing_Theory

283 Wanzer, M. B, A. B. Frymier, A. M. Wojtaszczyk & T. Smith (2006). Appropriate and inappropriate uses of humor by teachers, *Communication Education*, Vol. 55, No. 2, April 2006, pp. 178-196, retrieved on April 30, 2019 from https://www.researchgate.net/profile/Ann_Frymier/publication/240519126_Appropriate_and_Inappropriate_Uses_of_Humor_by_Teachers/links/544e34eb0cf2bca5ce8f1666/Appropriate-and-Inappropriate-Uses-of-Humor-by-Teachers.pdf?origin=publication_detail

Let us look at a few examples of instructional humor which are situated in-context.

> A mathematician organizes a lottery in which the prize is an infinite amount of money. When the winning ticket is drawn, and the jubilant winner comes to claim his prize, the mathematician explains the mode of payment: "1 dollar now, 1/2 dollar next week, 1/3 dollar the week after that..."[284]

This joke illustrates the mathematical concept of a harmonic series, which adds up to infinity, depicted by the equation:

$$\sum_{n=1}^{\infty} \frac{1}{n} = 1 + \frac{1}{2} + \frac{1}{3} + \frac{1}{4} + \frac{1}{5} + \cdots$$

In standard terms, a teacher could use a non-humorous problem statement, like this one:[285]

> One example of these is the 'worm on the rubber band'. Suppose that a worm crawls along an infinitely-elastic one-meter rubber band at the same time as the rubber band is uniformly stretched. If the worm travels 1 centimeter per minute and the band stretches 1 meter per minute, will the worm ever reach the end of the rubber band?

This problem has a detailed technical solution and the poor worm would probably end up taking over 1037 years to reach the end of the band! But the humorous first problem immediately engages you. It makes you smile at the ingenuity of the mathematician, and makes you wonder why this could result in an infinite amount when the fraction of money every week is reducing towards zero. It makes you sympathize with the poor winner who you think may have to wait an infinite amount of time.

---

284 Mathematical Humor, retrieved on 16 November 2017 from http://www.math.utah.edu/~cherk/mathjokes.html

285 Harmonic Series (Mathematics), Wikipedia, retrieved on 04 August, 2018 from https://en.wikipedia.org/wiki/Harmonic_series_(mathematics)

One cartoon[286] depicts Newton sitting at the base of an apple tree. When the apple falls on his head, he arrives at a different (botanical) conclusion – the stem of the apple is not permanently fixed to the tree.

Apart from its 'laugh value', what the cartoon illustrates is quite interesting. It introduces a personality called Newton, two scientific disciplines (Botany and Physics) and the power of observation in Science. It provokes us to think about the difference between disciplines – botany and physics – and how people can view the same phenomenon from different lenses. It also inspires us to ask what alternative perceptions could be. So a cartoon could be used not just to break the ice, but to also arouse curiosity and interest in the subject matter directly or indirectly.

Another cartoon[287] shows a tiny building adjacent to a huge building. The tiny building houses experts at genetic engineering. The huge building next to it focuses on ethics. It prompts us to see the imbalance between genetic engineering and the associated ethical implications. Genetic engineers could create situations which could have serious ethical consequences, requiring an incongruously larger effort to interpret and manage.

The second category - unrelated humor - accounted for most of the remaining examples (44 percent). The five most frequently identified types were stories (20 percent), jokes (17 percent), critical/cynical humor (14 percent), teasing students (14 percent), and college life stereotypes (14 percent). These made up 79 percent of the responses in this criterion. In the third category, self-disparaging humor, which made up 9 percent of the examples, 80 percent of the examples were classified in the personal characteristics (33 percent), non-specified comments (27 percent), and embarrassing stories (20 percent) subcategories.

---

286 Science Cartoons Plus, S Harris, retrieved on April 30, 2019 from http://www.sciencecartoonsplus.com/gallery/biology/bio11.gif

287 Ibid, http://www.sciencecartoonsplus.com/gallery/biology/bio05.gif

Mark Anderson has a website with cartoons on different topics. In one example,[288] a student in his English grammar class laughs away his own inability to make the subject-verb agreement by personifying them and enhancing the incongruity of his attempt by saying "my subject and verb have agreed to disagree!"

Or take this example (Figure 25) from a student response to the problem of finding the breadth of the rectangle in a math test.

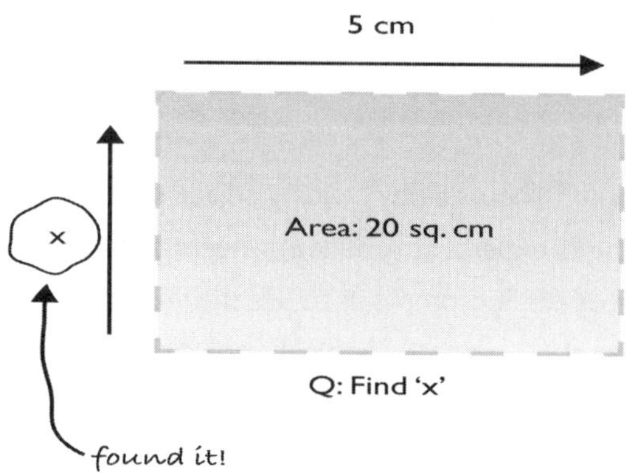


**Figure 25: Finding 'x' in a math test**

It is a funny, tongue-in-cheek response. It evokes laughter because of the incongruity it creates, and because it is so unexpectedly different from what you would expect to be done in this context.

Only 0.5 percent of the examples were slotted in the fourth category, unintentional humor, perhaps pointing at teachers being quite careful in their communications in this instance.

When looking at inappropriate humor, 42 percent of the examples fell into the 'disparaging humor: targeting students' category of which 83 percent examples involved targeting a specific student for reasons of

288 Teacher Cartoon #4009, Andertoons, retrieved on August 04, 2018 from https://www.andertoons.com/teacher/cartoon/4009/my-subject-and-verb-have-agreed-to-disagree

intelligence (26 percent), unspecified teasing, (24 percent) and student's personal life/opinions (17 percent). In 17 percent of the responses, when the professor disparaged students as a group, the largest subcategory was 'intelligence' (60 percent). The second category, 'disparaging humor: targeting others' (27 percent); largely (76 percent) a focus on gender (34 percent), race/ethnicity (31 percent), or university affiliations (11 percent). 30 percent of the examples were in the 'offensive humor' category with the top three subtypes (75 percent) being 'sexual comments and jokes' (35 percent), 'vulgar verbal and non-verbal expressions' (27 percent), and humor 'associated with drinking' (13 percent).

A preliminary study[289] based on the above classification of humor and its impact on effective learning, teacher perception and student-teacher relationships, finds that students' disposition towards humor is important when gauging their perception of humor. It was found that the greatest learning occurred when humor orientation (HO), defined as the degree to which someone appreciates, enacts and creates humor, was high in both the student and the teacher. High HO students may regard more types of humor as appropriate than others. Extraverts, defined as people who are outgoing, expressive and comfortable in interacting with their surroundings,[290] may have similar perceptions, and so could students who display a high degree of verbal aggression and possess effective communication skills, as they are better able to relate and differentiate between types of humor. Similar to student dispositions, students' perceptions of acceptable teacher behavior may also influence their perception of what appropriate teacher humor is. Inappropriate humor may impact teacher credibility.

289 Frymie, Ann Bainbridge, Melissa Bekelja Wanzer, Ann M. Wojtaszczyk (2007). Assessing student perceptions of inappropriate and appropriate teacher humor, November 2007, retrieved on November 19, 2017 from http://files.eric.ed.gov/fulltext/ED499080.pdf

290 Mind: Introverted vs. Extraverted, 16 Personalities, retrieved on November 19, 2017 https://www.16personalities.com/articles/mind-introverted-vs-extraverted

It is important to note that humor is not mandatory for effective instruction, but there is sufficient evidence from research that humor can positively impact learning outcomes, build positive student perceptions about the learning environment, heighten recall, and increase student attention and interest. Medical science also explains that humor acts at a physical level as well.[291]

> Moreover, humor stimulates multiple physiological systems that decrease levels of stress hormones, such as cortisol and epinephrine, and increase the activation of the mesolimbic dopaminergic reward system.

The research on humor in educational settings is important because it attempts to distinguish in practical terms, how humor is used and perceived in the classroom. While it may not be an exact science, and there will be differences in approaches, these can act as a reference point for teachers when thinking about humor as a strategy for the classroom. A teacher could use humor techniques that she and her students are comfortable with, rather than trying to force fit humor into every situation.

291 Savage, Brandon M., Heidi L. Lujan, Raghavendar R. Thipparthi, and Stephen E. DiCarlo (2017). Humor, laughter, learning, and health! A brief review, Department of Physiology, Wayne State University School of Medicine, Detroit, Michigan, submitted 6 March 2017; accepted in final form 29 March 2017, retrieved on August 04, 2018 from https://www.physiology.org/doi/10.1152/advan.00030.2017

# In Conclusion

> And how many hours a day did you do lessons?' said Alice, in a hurry to change the subject.
>
> 'Ten hours the first day,' said the Mock Turtle: 'nine the next, and so on.'
>
> 'What a curious plan!' exclaimed Alice.
>
> 'That's the reason they're called lessons,' the Gryphon remarked: 'because they lessen from day to day.
>
> *Alice in Wonderland*
> *– Lewis Carroll*

There are many ways the Lessons lessen in our systems of education. The *WhatIfs* in this book and those in your minds and hearts have the potential to halt or reverse that. What we should lessen instead are the challenges imposed on us by the educracy. And this can only happen by starting purposeful conversations around ideas such as the ones in this book.

If we care enough, and we should, the reflections, conversations and actions that we create around these themes could create a sustainable and lasting impact on our systems of education.

Our education systems need to benefit from the scale and diversity within which they thrive. For this to happen, a certain open plurality of thought and practice has to be engendered, and top-down educratic mandates have to fade into obscurity. It is incumbent upon you to make your reflections open, to bring your own perspective, experience and expertise to bear upon the problems at hand, and to collaboratively reflect on the quality of solutions designed to solve these problems.

The open, complex and adaptive nature of our education systems has to be studied deeply, if we are to harness it for our collective long term benefit. Designing for emergent behaviors is crucial if we want to re-envision the future. We cannot continue to impose deterministic outcomes on systems that are inherently chaotic.

It is my firm belief that the desired transformation will happen if we continue to ask such WhatIfs and implement what we learn from studying them, otherwise the lessons we learn will continue to lessen, until one day, we may have nothing more to learn.

# *About the Author*

**Viplav** is an education professional and researcher working at the interface between education and technology. Starting from the early 1990s, his work in K12, higher education and professional learning has spanned diverse themes such as digital pedagogy, serious games and simulations, Connectivism and MOOCs, and technologies underpinning large content and learning management systems.

The Book's Hashtag: #whatifedu
Web: http://www.whatifedu.com
Twitter: https://twitter.com/whatifedubook
Facebook: https://www.facebook.com/WhatifEdubook/

**Reach Viplav at:**

Blog: http://learnos.wordpress.com
Twitter: @viplavbaxi
LinkedIn: www.linkedin.com/in/vbaxi